car•pe a•qua•lis (car' pay ah' kwa lis)

[Latin derivative: carpe, *seize* + aqualis, *wave.*]

1. *(verb)* Taking full advantage of skills, talents, abilities and attitudes to convert challenges into opportunities and victories.

2. *(noun)* Powerful combination of opportunity awareness grounded in the realization of ultimate personal responsibility. See also: *"Your World. Your Wave!"*

3. *(adjective)* To represent a person or organization applying full measure of creativity and adaptability regardless of the situation.

4. *(interjection/expression/battle cry) Carpe Aqualis!*

Advance Praise for
Carpe Aqualis! Seize the Wave

"Incredible! Frank Lunn reveals an entrepreneurial tool kit to immediately convert change and stress into beneficial opportunities. Get *Carpe Aqualis!* today to seize your wave and surf the rich life that awaits you!"
–**David M. Frees III, Esq.** CEO, SuccessTechnologies™ Inc. and author of *The Language of Parenting: Building Great Family Relationships at All Ages*

"Unlike any other, this book gets you ready to paddle hard toward the next wave in your life. Frank Lunn takes you on a powerful ride; his words will touch your heart, strengthen your courage, and stoke your enthusiasm."
–**John D. Clatworthy**, Vice President of Sales & Marketing, Cash Connect by WSFS Bank

"*Carpe Aqualis!* is a wonderful fast-paced book, loaded with principles and inspiration for success and achievement in every part of life."
–**Thomas J. Arkell**, Attorney, Dunn, Willard, Arkell & Bugg

"Thanks Frank for another 'Outstanding!' book. *Carpe Aqualis!* is a great business enhancing book, and more importantly, a life enhancing book with timeless wisdom and inspiration. It deserves to be read by all."
–**Randy Gilbert**, host of "The Inside Success Show"

"Everyone hits unexpected turbulence at one time or another. Read *Carpe Aqualis!* to uncover invaluable tools for meeting life's challenges head on! Live it to meet life's opportunities with joy and strength!"
–**Carolina Fernandez**, Author of *ROCKET MOM! 7 Strategies To Blast You Into Brilliance*

"This book ROCKS!!! *Carpe Aqualis!* is the new battle cry for finding and surfing opportunity all around us!"
–**Tom Antion**, Professional Speaker and Trainer

"Instead of telling you why others are to blame for your failure, Frank gives you insight into how you may succeed. *Carpe Aqualis!* gives you the keys and insights that you need to thrive."
–**David Soper**, Dean of Men, Cincinnati Christian University

"Frank's practical approach and ability to distill meaningful truths into powerful lessons makes this book one of the most pragmatic I have ever read. Pray your competitors don't read *Carpe Aqualis!*"
–**Darryl Ware**, President, WWS, Inc.

"A powerful guide to success! This book will help you leave the shore and seize the waves that come your way... your life will never be the same."
–**David Cottrell**, President, CornerStone Leadership Institute and author of *Monday Morning Leadership*

"Frank reveals a high impact approach to mastering change. *Carpe Aqualis!* will teach you how to surf for success. Read it! Live it! And by all means–Ride The Wave!"
–**Roger Pryor**, President, Sharpening The Edge Ministries

"Frank Lunn has done it again! Clear steps to take in navigating through life's most challenging moments — change and disappointment. A brilliant process out of the abyss that propels you into positive action. Rethink what you can do and what is truly possible with this gratifying guide."
–**Samantha Guthrie**, President, AATMS, Inc.

"Ready to break free from the obstacles holding you back? *Carpe Aqualis!* is full of new insights and inspiration to prevent the paralysis of negative thinking - this isn't a book to read, it is one to live!"
–**Steve Barnhart**, Eagle Rock Consulting, Leadership Team Coach and Author of Business Blueprints! Leadership Simplified, Results Multiplied

"The waves of life are full of uncertainty... Dive into the power-packed S.U.R.F. Strategy to discover how to be your own 'Big Kahuna.'"
–**Roy Giorgi**, President, Infrastructure Systems, Inc.

"This book is a powerful wake up call for who we can become and how to get the most out of life."
–**Rick Schaltegger**, Attorney

"If you have ever asked the question, how can I give *myself* a promotion, here is your answer! Frank's S.U.R.F. Strategy cuts straight to the heart of riding change to new opportunities. Quick wit and humor make this book worth reading again and again!"
–**Rick Frishman**, President, Planned Television Arts, a division of Ruder-Finn and Bestselling author of Networking Magic

"Frank eloquently captures the reality of his personal leadership style and shares it in an engaging and thoughtful manner. This is a book that is truly more than a book - it is a new way of liberating your potential!"
–**Rick Galbreath**, President, Human Resources Growth Partners Inc.

"Informative and sharply written, *Carpe Aqualis!* is a must read. Sometimes life throws you powerful waves, but your options are clear: take control of your future and succeed on your own terms, with hope, knowledge and a positive attitude!"
–**Michael F. Giorgi**, Vice President, Infrastructure Systems, Inc.

"*Carpe Aqualis!* is the 'riptionary' of life! Frank's vision teaches us to not just surf but embrace the waves, turning turbulence into an effective lifetime. This book is our boogie board in a rapidly changing world."
–**Tracy Davis-Pitts**, Vice President, Suzi Davis Travel Ltd.

"Frank, you certainly have your readers surf board pointed in the right direction... thanks for a great book."
–**C.W. "Al" Allen**, President and CEO, Corporate Alternatives, Inc.

"Frank Lunn masters the uncertainty of the ocean as compared to daily life. *Carpe Aqualis!* is a simple and effective guide enabling us to be on top of life's waves instead of being a constant victim of them. It's true – we will seize the day when we learn to seize the wave!"
–**Randy Clay**, Bestselling author, *Small Business Swimming Lessons with Sharkmaster, Jr.*

Carpe Aqualis!SM
"Seize the Wave"

7 ESSENTIAL SURFING SKILLS TO REVOLUTIONIZE YOUR BUSINESS AND PERSONAL LIFE

FRANK F. LUNN
AUTHOR OF STACK THE LOGS!
BUILDING A SUCCESS FRAMEWORK TO REACH YOUR DREAMS

Kahuna Empowerment, Incorporated
801 W. Chestnut Street, Suite C
Bloomington, IL 61701
www.KahunaPower.com

Although the author and publisher have made every effort to ensure the accuracy and completeness of information contained in this book, we assume no responsibility for errors, inaccuracies, omissions, or any inconsistency herein. Any slights of people, places, or organizations are unintentional.

First printing 2006
ISBN 0-9728300-7-3
LCCN 2005928246

The following terms are the trademarked property of Frank F. Lunn and Kahuna Empowerment, Incorporated:

Carpe Aqualis
S.U.R.F. Strategy
S.T.A.C.K. Strategy
Stack The Logs!
Terro-Phoria
P.L.F. (Perspective Learning Forward)
Surf-Titude
Your World. Your Wave!
Stewardship Pyramid
No-Wave Thinking
Blessings in Adversity

Attention corporations, universities, colleges, and professional organizations! Quantity discounts are available on bulk purchases of this book for educational, gift purposes, or as premiums for increasing magazine subscriptions or renewals. Special books or book excerpts may also be created to fit specific needs. For information, please contact Kahuna Empowerment, Inc., 801 W. Chestnut Street, Suite C, Bloomington, IL 61701, call 309-828-8396, or visit:

www.CarpeAqualis.com and www.KahunaPower.com

Dedication

We proudly dedicate this book to the creation of the Kahuna Charitable Foundation, a 501(c)(3) not-for-profit corporation created to support St. Jude Children's Research Hospital in their mission of: *"Finding cures. Saving children."* www.KahunaCharitable.org

This endeavor would not be possible without the belief and unconditional support of my "All4One" Kahuna business partners and each one of our Carpe Aqualis! Kahuna teammates who surf with us every day. I am privileged, honored and extremely humbled to be your leader. I thank you all for your inspiration and your dedication in every aspect of living our mission and vision and building our growing business through Leverage, Value, Partnership and "Achieving our victories through the victories of those we serve."

Acknowledgements

I am excited about graduating from a single concept to help others and raise money for St. Jude Children's Research Hospital to a division of Kahuna, to the newly created Kahuna Empowerment Inc. and our growing opportunity to serve others. I truly appreciate Stacy Laffere and Jason Ficks for your belief in our vision and in joining our team to take KahunaPower.com and our Kahuna Empowerment mission to the next level—it will be a tremendous journey. Of course, none of this would be possible without the leadership, consistent hard work and dedication of Timothy Bill; thank you for your friendship and service in helping us get this far. Thanks also to Nicole Williams for your efforts and assistance in launching our vision.

To my dear friends and Kahuna business partners Tom Mortimer, Ernie Beckman, Jason Sharpe, Scott Rathbun and Tammy Cook: thank you for your support and belief in the mission of Kahuna Empowerment and allowing me the freedom and opportunity to pursue it.

To Bryan Bauer and every member of Team Kahuna: I give thanks for your steady leverage, value and partnership with our clients in our core business. Your example was present in every part of this book creation.

Thank you to all the clients, vendor partners and friends of Kahuna ATM Solutions who have helped us grow. There are so many others, but a special note of thanks to my good friends Roger Mogan and Darryl Ware at WWS. You have been with us from the very beginning and I am thankful for the journey together.

Thank you to my friends John and Kim Wohlwend who believed in me and helped us through the many early lessons learned as we birthed the Empowerment Division. A special thank you to Christi Sands for your friendship and for all of your selfless help during Frankie's illness and recovery.

To our friends, peers and mentors who freely share their support: we appreciate being on this journey together and are proud to be in your company. The list is too numerous to mention by name, but we would specifically like to thank you for all you have done to help us achieve our mission with St. Jude Children's Research Hospital and in changing lives.

Thank you Maria Griffin, Pat Adams and the rest of the team at my early morning writing office at Denny's® in Bloomington. Thanks for your encouragement, keeping my coffee full and providing me with space to get work done before the day gets crazy.

Thank you to my extended family of the Millers and Robinsons, Mom and R.K. for your love and support in all things. I am thankful for the memory and example of selfless service and humility of my mother-in-law, Claudia Robinson, who sadly passed from this world in 2004. I also acknowledge my late father, Frank III, for the legacy he entrusted to me.

To my wonderful wife, Lisa, and our young surfer kids Frankie, Matthew and Rachel: thank you for putting up with my crazy schedule and for your unwavering love and support. I am blessed beyond belief and thank God every day for his gift of our Ohana team. I love you all with all my heart!

I would like to thank the congregation at LeRoy Christian Church, my pastor Tim Vollstedt, and all my brothers and sisters in Christ who pray for me to keep me grounded in my faith. Thanks for being on this journey with me. Above all, I give thanks to my Lord and Savior Jesus Christ who gave his life so that I may have eternal salvation. I am proud to be a Carpe Aqualis! Christian (a future book release, and like me, a work in progress).

Mahalo and blessings to all!

Frank F. Lunn IV
Bloomington, Illinois
May, 2005

Table of Contents

Preface

Dear Friend,

This is <u>NOT</u> another "how to deal with change" book. Brace yourself... this is a "how to master change survival course!" When problems, obstacles, challenges and opportunities come at you from every angle with increasing magnitude, you will learn the secret of the S.U.R.F.™ Strategy to gain an advantage in each of these situations. In the pages that follow, you will develop the mind-set and secret language of an entrepreneur. *Carpe Aqualis!* will equip you with seven essential surfing skills guaranteed to revolutionize your business and personal life! More than concepts and theories, this book hands you the tools and practical insight that you can apply immediately to your life. Do not settle for dealing with change... take control and master it! After reading this book, you will be transformed. You will never look at change with anxiety and fear again!

Learn to Embrace Terro-Phoria™

Have you ever been on a roller coaster or thrill ride? If so, you might recognize that emotion somewhere between terror and euphoria. I call this Terro-Phoria™. Terro-Phoria describes business opportunities or other changes so big they scare us but at the same time excite us. Terro-Phoria is the same emotion shared by big wave surfers and Wall Street traders. It is experienced by bungee jumpers and skydivers — and by mothers seeing their kids off to school for the first time. Once the roller coaster has started, it is too late to back down. The only real option is to embrace Terro-Phoria, learn skills to improve your ability to ride the changes and maintain a *Carpe Aqualis!* attitude.

You Can't Control the Waves, Only How You Surf

Make no mistake - both real and metaphorical surfing are skills. It takes time to accept the waves life has given you and adapt to them. Take heart; no matter how old or young you are, no matter what your level of education or training is, you can develop the surfer mind-set. You can survive and thrive no matter what the waves bring. *Carpe Aqualis!* Seize the Wave! Bring it on!

Chapter 0

Begin Your Journey Here

Surf -Titude:

"You cannot control the waves, but you can control your response to them...and that is really all that matters."

We may not know each other yet, but there are a few things I know about your life. I know the next several years will be very different from the previous ones. The world around you is changing at a pace never before experienced. Changes in science, technology, culture and education are forever evolving your world. Things that were revolutionary yesterday will be outdated tomorrow. Skills learned five years ago may be obsolete. As we are bombarded with information, we're asked to process it faster and produce more than ever before.

I remember reading a book called *Future Shock* by Alvin Toffler. The title comes from a condition he described as "future-shock syndrome," where massive and rapid rates of change potentially cause physical ailments or breakdowns in much the same way a soldier returning from battle might suffer from post-traumatic stress disorder.

The world is changing and the rate of change is picking up speed. I am, as of this writing, approaching my thirty-ninth birthday. When I went to school twenty years ago, things were very different. I remember carrying a twelve-gauge shotgun down the hall of my school where I met fifteen other boys with shotguns to go to a shooting range as part of the sportsman's club. Today, after the tragedy of Columbine High School? Unimaginable!

There were no cell phones or pagers in our classrooms for good reason; the first cell phones were the size of backpacks. Our first microwave ovens took forever and left some of the food raw and the rest nuked beyond recognition. We did not have a TV remote control until my senior year and got our first VCR about the same time. Now there are VCRs, DVRs, DVDs, and screens as big as most theaters. And of course, back then there was no Internet. We actually used dictionaries and encyclopedias to write our papers.

My first computer had 56K of memory and a dot matrix printer. My six-year-old daughter has a little reading and speaking computer with more than ten times that computing power. The computing power in your cell phone is greater than the computing power for the Apollo 11 mission! Instead of PlayStation® or XBox®, we had Pong, or if we were lucky, Atari®. I think you're getting the picture. In two decades, the world has completely remade itself technologically.

Most experts agree that the amount of known information is doubling every five to seven years. Within the next fifteen years, it is predicted that known information will double every seventy-three days. Today's Internet is thought to be doubling in size every 250-300 days, with the number of websites doubling every three months! E-zines and online publishing make any information on any subject immediately available. And with this massive increase in real and relevant information comes a corresponding increase in "junk" information - SPAM, unsolicited e-mails, advertisements and more. Talk about information overload!

Modern society is running on a treadmill. Stress comes in the realization of the increasing pace and the feeling of not being able to keep up. Technology reduces the amount of time it takes to do something while increasing our work capacity and expanding what's expected of us. We are connected like never before with global positioning satellites, two-way pagers, cell phones, DSL, wireless Internet and e-mail. You can be sunning yourself on a remote island in the Caribbean but the home office can still reach you. Connectivity is both our blessing and our curse.

Life has never been easier, yet more people are on medication - prescribed, imbibed, legal and otherwise. Reading the paper recently, I highlighted the words apathy, anger, despair, worry, anxiety, fear, depression, aggression, helplessness, burnout, tension and irritation in a single article related to workers and change in the new global economy. Change is unforeseeable and unavoidable. It takes away our feeling of control. When we feel out of control, it causes stress and anxiety. Have you ever experienced this? Are you experiencing this today as the rate of change keeps increasing?

There is a Solution

Life is in a constant state of change. This is reality. These changes, like the waves of the ocean, are both constant and unpredictable. In life, there are really only two types of waves - challenges and opportunities. Both have the power to wipe you out or give you a tremendous ride. The only difference really is in your approach... an approach you have the power to choose!

Carpe Aqualis! Seize the Wave

In the movie *Dead Poets Society*, Robin Williams, who plays a teacher shouts out, "Carpe Diem!" (which roughly translated means to "seize the day") to his young students, challenging them to not just accept life but to boldly capture it and live it to the fullest.

A similar idea is the key to embracing change. But first, let me tell you something you may not have known about yourself: you are a surfer. You live at a point in history where we are seeing the most dramatic waves of change. Everything about your world is changing: technology, communication, travel, business, health, relationships... the list goes on and on. For the rest of your life, you will be in a situation where you will be constantly learning, unlearning, relearning, adapting and changing to fit into the world around you. The world is washed by endless waves of change, and like it or not, you are surfing.

You may not buy into this completely, but ignoring the wave will not make it go away any more than not believing in the law of gravity will keep you from landing on your butt when you fall. As any surfer will tell you, big waves leave you with only three choices.

1. Ignore them... and get blind-sided;
2. Fight them... and get battered; or
3. Learn to surf! Take whatever comes your way and make the best of it. Apply your skills, attitude, talents and ambition to turn change into opportunity.

Surfing is about dealing with and adapting to change. Ultimately, surfing is about survival. Think about it. For a surfer, what would be a life-threatening situation for another person - a giant wave about to crash down - becomes a source of propulsion, energy, and joy. *Carpe Aqualis!* Seize the wave. It means making the most of the changes and upheaval in your life.

Surfers are optimistic. They learn to see opportunity within the waves of change. In our journey, we will explore practical ways to apply this to any situation. You will be amazed at how your worldview changes when you approach every new challenge as an opportunity to surf and test your skills against the waves. Surfers don't have a goal to ride easier and easier waves. The better they become, the bigger the challenges are that they seek. When you accept the challenges thrown at you as opportunities, you will start looking for new and innovative ways to test yourself.

Get Ready to Seize YOUR Wave

The world is more challenging than ever before. There is also more opportunity than ever before. There has never been a better time or a better chance to change your economic and social condition. Education is at your fingertips. The connected global economy opens up a world of possibilities. Your station in life and your rewards are in your control more today than ever before in the history of humankind.

Don't ignore change. Don't fight it. Embrace it and learn to surf! Carpe Aqualis! Seize your wave and create your own future. While everyone else complains about the waves, you will have a massive advantage and your life will never be the same. You cannot control the waves, but you can control your response to them... and that is really all that matters.

Surf -Titude:

"Great opportunities never come to those who wait; they are captured by those who learn to surf!"

Chapter 1

Your Security is Not in the Wave - It's in Your Ability to Surf!

Surf -Titude:

"Seize the opportunities created in change! Carpe Aqualis! Seize the wave."

Are you living the life you always dreamed? Are you experiencing the best in your family, career, relationships? Do you wake up every day with a passion for what you are doing and for the challenges in your life? Do you look upon the future with optimism and excitement?

My hunch is that you might not be able to answer a resounding "Yes!" to all of the above. If you are like most people, your true feelings might have tied a knot in your stomach. Most people are in a rut, which I have heard defined as a grave with the ends kicked out. They do the zombie shuffle to and from work every day without passion or purpose. Sound familiar?

By the end of this book, you will definitely and truthfully answer yes to each of these questions. You will transition into a world of abundance and possibilities because you are going to learn a new language. It may sound like the language you already speak, but do not be fooled, it's very different indeed.

The Language of Opportunity

In the movie *The Sixth Sense*, the little boy delivers the most memorable line of the entire movie: "I see dead people... they're everywhere." I feel like that little boy when I say, "I see opportunities... they're everywhere!"

One of my business partners is bilingual. He and his wife are fluent in English and Spanish. Sometimes when they talk, they effortlessly slip in and out of one language into another. I made a decision to become conversationally fluent in Spanish. Although I'm far from fluent as of this writing, I can pick up a few words and phrases. The more I learn, the more I can converse and move around comfortably within the language. The more I share dialogue with others in the language, the faster my proficiency increases.

My second language is *opportunity*. I speak it fluently with other entrepreneurs and people of the same mind-set. If you were to overhear a conversation between me and one of my colleagues, it might be as foreign to you as Spanish originally was to me. But there is nothing overly complicated about it. It is a subtle language filled with hidden meaning, almost a code.

Here are some examples. Most people talk about problems as *hardships* and difficulties. I don't like problems any more than the next person, but I like *challenges* and I love *opportunities*. By changing my vocabulary, I get a different perspective. This new approach allows me to attack challenges and capitalize on opportunities, rather than avoiding and stressing over problems.

If you have a fever and are prescribed medicine, a reaction is not what the doctor desires. Instead, the doctor expects the body to respond to the prescribed medicine. *Reaction* implies that control has been taken away from you whereas the word *respond* offers more choices. When an elite athlete is in a stressful competition, she doesn't want to *react*. She wants to *respond*. Reaction is out of her control; responding is under her control. Learning to respond to situations rather than react to them is a subtle skill that can make a big difference in your outcomes.

You may have two questions in your mind right about now:

1. Why should I care about this?
2. What makes you an expert?

Good questions. Let's look at the first one. You should care because you have the potential to become a "life entrepreneur," a surfer fluent in the language of opportunity. Your Carpe Aqualis! skill-set will allow you to seize opportunities others don't see – or run away from. Success in your career, marriage, and beyond is based on your ability to find and respond to opportunities, regardless of the circumstances. As you learn to speak and apply the language of opportunity as a life entrepreneur, you will see things others do not see. You'll see dramatic improvements in your life as your stress is converted into exhilaration.

What makes me an expert? I'm not. No one is. I am, however, a committed, lifelong student of entrepreneurship and human psychology. I'm blessed with tremendous curiosity and I have spent my adult life focused on finding and creating opportunities. I am a college dropout, yet I've been privileged to be part of a business team that has created more than $25 million in revenue every year... and is still growing. I am trained to speak and translate opportunity. These opportunities are all around you and have never been more attainable than right now.

Surfing the Waves of Change

When waves of change hit, you have two choices for responding. The choice you make will determine your outcome.

1. You choose to react negatively. The outcome: difficulty and strife that diminish your future prospects.
2. You choose to react with optimism and positive action. The outcome: opportunity and the potential for prosperity, achievement and a positive future. *Carpe Aqualis!* is a mind-set.

Congratulations! Today you've become a surfer. By beginning to respond to the waves (change) with a sense of possibility and optimism, you are becoming a life entrepreneur. The *American Heritage® Dictionary* defines an **en · tre · pre · neur** as: "A person who organizes, operates, and assumes the risk for a business venture." An entrepreneur can sometimes be described as a visionary self-starter who loves the adventure of a new enterprise. You might be thinking that this does not apply to you. Isn't being an entrepreneur about getting a loan and opening a restaurant or something? It can be. But at the most basic level, being an entrepreneur is about creation and innovation. Those are forces you can use to shape your future.

Look at yourself as a business. If you have a job, aren't you organizing, operating, and assuming risk? What's the difference between that and starting your own medical practice or Internet company? The only difference is the perception of your security.

I have been an entrepreneur as long as I can remember from the lemonade stand to lawn mowing to the candle making shop I had at eight years old. People tell me they would love to start a business but are too afraid of giving up their security. I would argue that as an entrepreneur, I have more security than they do. I am in control of my prosperity and my welfare. I can diversify my business among as many clients as I wish to ensure that I can withstand economic ups and downs. I have the privilege of working with many clients. Someone with a job only has one client. I am certainly not trying to convince you to quit your job to start a business. I just want to challenge the myth of security in any job.

Your security is NOT in the company you work for. Your security is not in your boss, your industry, your geography, the government or in any social program. Your career security is in you.

Surf -Titude:

"God provides the waves. What you do with those waves is up to you!"

Your World. Your Wave!™

Surfing is ultimately about personal responsibility. There's a saying that goes, "If it is to be, it is up to me!" We have adapted this to become, "Your World. Your Wave!" This is the recognition of total personal responsibility for your life. At the end of the day, no one else is going to get it done for you... it is your world and it is your wave. Surfing is an individual sport; life is no different. Like life, surfing is certainly more enjoyable when you are part of a larger community, but no matter how supportive others are, only you can take on your wave. Realizing this is absolutely liberating. If you are looking for your mom, dad, sister, brother, spouse, best friend, boss, coach, counselor, teacher, therapist, government, and so on to do it for you, guess what? It will not happen. You are the only one who can surf the waves you are given.

Opportunity is optimism with a plan; it is creativity applied to the future. There is a saying, "He who is good with a hammer sees every problem as a nail." I want you to see opportunity in almost everything and to channel that opportunity obsession to areas consistent with your long-term vision, goals and plans.

No Matter Who You Work for, YOU Are the Boss of YOU!

If someone asks you who your boss is, do you think of someone else? Perhaps a supervisor at work? The reality is that *you* are the only boss of *you*. You are the only person who can live your life, and you are the only one in control of direction and results. Change is constant. It is important to realize we are constantly changing. Think about the era in which we live. Thanks to technology and communication, this is the first time in the history of the world that you have the ability to choose what you want to be, where you want to go and how you want to live. This is an unprecedented freedom and most people take it for granted. Either they don't see it or it terrifies them. If you're going to become an accomplished surfer of change, you've got to see this freedom and embrace it. You've got to accept that nobody is going to shape your life for you. The power –and the responsibility –is completely yours.

The Root of Freedom Is Responsibility

There is no freedom without responsibility. The more freedom you have, the more the responsibility increases. Think about a new baby. She has no freedom and no responsibility. Her parents take care of all of her needs. When she becomes a young child and gets her first taste of freedom, there are rules and some boundaries that cannot be violated, all for her safety. When she becomes a teenager, she's dying to be free of parental control, but she isn't mature enough to understand that responsibility follows freedom like a shadow. Freedom loses a bit of its luster when you realize it comes with a cost: finding a job, paying rent, buying food and clothing, and obeying laws.

The cornerstone of your character is the personal responsibility upon which the rest of your life will be built. Personal responsibility is essential to the foundation of your character and your integrity. If you are free to create your own future, you must be responsible for it as well.

Responsibility is the currency of freedom. Those who are deficient in personal responsibility always seem to blame others and look for scapegoats. Scapegoating surrenders your power to someone else. Accepting responsibility in your life and in creating your future gives you power.

General Douglas MacArthur rightly observed, "There is no security in this life. There is only opportunity." Circumstances and luck do not really play a part in long-term success. Actions and choices produce results; otherwise how would two children raised in identical family circumstances turn out differently? How can some children who grow up in poverty break the cycle while others perpetuate it?

The more people seek security, the further it retreats. Ironically, playing it safe is the greatest risk you can take. There is no such thing as job security. The only security is in your talents, skills and adaptability to the situation around you. If you are looking for a job or another person to give you security, you will be disappointed.

Carpe Aqualis! is a battle cry. It is a mind-set and an approach to life. It is also a skill-set that can be learned. It is a resolution to not just let life happen but rather to learn to surf the waves and adapt to the circumstances that confront you. *Carpe Aqualis!* is a movement and a revolution. Most of all, it's a call to action. It is a call to convert life's challenges into life's opportunities.

Surf -Titude:

"To be a Carpe Aqualis! surfer, make sure your dreams are bigger than your fears!"

Chapter 2
A Rising Tide Lifts All Surfboards

Surf-Titude:

"The better surfer you are, the less you have to tell others. It is demonstrated in your actions and attitudes. The higher you go in any organization, the more humble you need to be."

True Success Comes from Openness

If you get only one thing from this book, I sincerely hope you understand that your success will come from bringing value or service to other people. This is the essence of opportunity, but it's difficult for some people to find. As a culture, we are trained to be self-centered. This does not lead to a life of abundance.

When I was younger, I looked for all kinds of short-cut, get-rich-quick schemes with the goal of making money. I wasn't doing anything unethical or illegal, but I was missing the most important aspect of building wealth. When I finally figured it out, my financial situation changed and my life was enhanced. Looking back, it amazes me how simple the answer was. Allow me to save you the years and the frustration. The answer is so simple you need to be careful not to miss its magnitude. It is only a few words, but like a small key, it will unlock a very big door.

What you give... you get.

This is the law of reciprocity. Give to get. If you want to get rich, first enrich others. A farmer doesn't plant beans and expect corn to grow. Only what is planted can be harvested. Give away freely whatever you want and it will return to you. When you give your time, time will come back to you. To get respect, give respect. To get love, give love. Give value, praise, freedom and the same will return to you.

By the same token, holding onto something out of greed or jealousy will choke its freedom to grow. People who value money so much that they refuse to share it ironically diminish their ability to have even more money. Your life is an investment – if heartache and bitterness are your dividends, what was your initial deposit?

Caught in a Spin

When I first started learning to fly an airplane, my instructor performed a stall maneuver to test my proficiency in an emergency situation. He pulled back the yoke, which raised the nose of the aircraft to a steep angle and slowed us down to a crawl. Losing air speed over the wings, the plane seemed to stand still, shake violently and then the shrill stall-warning alarm sounded. Talk about stress. The plane began to fall like a rock with the nose pointing about forty-five degrees down, spinning on a collision course with terra firma. Every instinct in my body screamed to pull back on the yoke to lift the nose of the airplane. Doing this, however, would have further reduced air speed over the wings and could have potentially left us in a deadly flat spin.

Instead, I followed my training and pushed the yoke forward. Counter to my instincts, this action increased air speed over the wings and stopped us from spinning and falling. I was able to regain control and resume straight and level flight.

Our culture tells you that to be successful, you must consume, take care of number one, don't give or people will want more, and on and on. The reality is different.

Opportunity is not found in, "what's in it for me?" Instead it should be, "How can I give value to others?" Bill Gates is the richest man in the world because of the value he added for billions of computer users. Musicians, actors and athletes get paid big money based on the value they add.

Getting Value by Giving Value

In 1989, I heard Zig Ziglar say, "You can have anything in life you want if you just help enough other people get what they want." It hit me like a ton of bricks. I did not know how to apply it then, but it made real sense and changed my approach to business. Today, Kahuna Business Group has a simple mission with regard to our business endeavors and our relationships with our clients: "Business development through Leverage, Value and Partnership! We achieve our victories through the victories of those we serve!" Our vision is: "Enterprise Focused. Opportunity Driven. Carpe Aqualis!" We are in a service business built around the business model of adding leverage, delivering value, and developing partnership with our clients. For us to get more, we need to give more.

Have you ever been on a winning team? How about just a fan of one? Winning is exhilarating, even if all you did was cheer. A rising tide lifts all surfboards. Whatever you do to add value in your community (family, work, neighborhood, church, and so on) ultimately brings value back to you. Surfing is an individual activity. No one else can surf for you. But there is a set of rules that must be followed to allow all surfers to safely coexist. Life, ultimately, is a team sport. You can't succeed unless you give to others more than they give to you.

The Truest Victories are Ones Achieved Through Others

Lunn! Get your sorry butt over here right now! What are you doing? Did you not listen to a word I said? Drop and give me twenty! What are you lookin

*at? Are you stupid or did your Mamma drop you
on your head as a child? You WILL go back and do
it again and this time you will do it like you are a
soldier. You have ten seconds to get out of my face
and eight of them are already gone! Now move it!*

Not exactly what you would expect in a nurturing and
caring relationship, but these very words (plus a few
more colorful ones) from Staff Sergeant Brown during the
hottest days of August in 1986 at Fort Benning, Georgia,
stand out vividly in my memory. Yes, Sergeant Brown
was my Airborne drill sergeant and although you might
not be able to tell from this excerpt, Sergeant Brown was
a tremendous teacher who made me a better soldier. His
methods were extreme because the nature of war and
jumping out of airplanes is extreme. Sergeant Brown
achieved his victories through my victories and the
victories of countless other soldiers. The drill instructors
from every branch of the military can take great pride
in the knowledge that their mission was accomplished
through those they trained.

Success, knowledge, love, respect and consideration are
never diminished when shared with others. When the
flame on the wick of a candle touches another wick, the
flame is not diminished. It is magnified as it is shared. Your
success and happiness will come in proportion to what you
add. This is true in families, workplaces, churches, in the
military, on sports teams and beyond. The strength of any
organization lies in the willingness of each member to give
everything for the team's benefit.

Your success is never diminished when you add value
to others. Isn't that the ultimate goal for coaches, teachers,
mentors, managers, supervisors and even drill sergeants?
Isn't this the main goal of parents as they nurture their
children? My victory as an author and teacher comes from
the victories of those who apply these concepts to achieve
greater success.

Aesop's Fable of the Father and His Sons

Aesop was a Greek slave who lived more than half a century before Christ. His truths and insights into human nature and behavior are as relevant today as they were three thousand years ago. And although he lived before surfing, I think he'd get it, as you can see from this fable:

> *A father had sons who were continuously quarreling. When his pleadings failed to mend their disputes, he decided to give them a practical illustration of the danger inherent in their lack of unity. One day, he told them to bring him a bundle of sticks. After they had done so, he gave each son the stick bundle, ordering each to break it in pieces. Not one was able to do it. The father then opened the bundle, took out the sticks individually, and one at a time placed them into the hands of his sons. This time the sons were able to easily break the sticks. Then he said to them. "My sons, if you are of one mind, and unite to fully assist each other, you will be as this bundle of wood, uninjured by all the attempts of your enemies. But if you are divided among yourselves, you will be broken as easily as these sticks."*

A rising tide lifts all surfboards and surfers. When you selflessly help others, your effort returns to you many times over in success, satisfaction and prosperity.

Surf-Titude:

"Define yourself with your actions. Your 'can do' attitude will be contagious and lift all surfboards!"

Chapter 3

The S.U.R.F. Strategy™ and 7 Essential Rules for Surfing Success

Surf -Titude:

"Opportunity is optimism with a plan creatively applied to the future."

Surfing as a Success Strategy

Success is an overused word, but it is really quite simple. Success is when you know where you want to go and you are taking meaningful action to get there. Earl Nightingale defined it as: "The progressive realization of a worthy goal." Success as a strategy is also very simple. You will have change in your life as certain as the waves will roll in from the ocean. Some changes are planned and welcome, whereas others will be unforeseen and potentially unwelcome. Your response to the changes and the conversion of them into opportunities will be the measure of your success. Your success in life (as you define it) will ultimately be a reflection of your ability to seize the opportunities created in change. In business and in your personal life, change will present either difficulties and hardship or opportunities to be converted into benefits for your life. The choice is yours.

If it was announced today that your company had been sold and was under new ownership effective in thirty days, how would you feel? It would be natural to feel some apprehension about the unknown. After a short period of reflection, you need to move forward and assess the situation for opportunities. What are your choices? You can be disgruntled and a malcontent, creating the stage for a negative, self-fulfilling prophecy. But, you also have the opportunity for a fresh start, applying new ideas to creating a new chapter in your career. The situation as presented is neutral. Your choices, ensuing actions and attitudes will create your new reality. Is there a chance the new situation might be worse? Of course, but if it is bad, it will be that way anyway without any help from you.

Surfing Terro-Phoria

Imagine yourself as a surfer. You know you're good. You're absolutely ready with a *Carpe Aqualis!* mind-set of: "Bring it on!" You have been preparing and putting yourself in position to ride the next big wave. You have trained yourself to recognize the ocean's signs that the next big wave is on its way. Suddenly, you feel the change in the ocean and the movement of the water. You see the towering wave approaching and your training kicks in. You begin to paddle like crazy, creating your own momentum before the massive swell arrives. As your energy converts to speed and the speed you produce is accelerated by the force of the water, you begin to lift. You push up into a low crouch, feeling the board latch onto the power of the wave, building momentum like a bicycle moving fast enough to stay up on its own.

Now your movements seem to be in slow motion, as every fiber of your being is tuned in to the wave – and more importantly – where the wave is taking you. Every muscle works to keep you on the board and moving toward your destination. The wave is at its peak and you experience the mixture of sheer terror and pure adrenaline excitement. Welcome to Terro-Phoria. That's a feeling you must learn to love – the terror and thrill of being challenged by opportunities so big they defy your imagination.

Surfing is both skill and attitude. Skill because it takes craft and practice to ride the waves. Attitude because you have to accept that you can ride the wave, but you can't affect it. Surfing is the perfect metaphor for dealing with change. Surfing is about flexibility and creative adaptability. It is the ability to take what is given to you and make the best of it. Don't adapt to change... MASTER IT!

Learning to S.U.R.F. Change

Change will happen. Your only point of control is the surfing skill-set you develop to adapt and make the best out of whatever comes your way. Remember, in every situation, it is not what happens to you as much as it is your response to what happens that matters. Your response determines your outcome. Think of change as waves and consider how you will respond to that wave. Success is not necessarily in your talents and abilities but in the choices you make in application to the waves.

Surf -Titude:

"When life gives you waves...
Learn to surf!"

Apply the S.U.R.F. Strategy™ to Make the Best of the Waves

The S.U.R.F. Strategy is a simple, quick strategy to adapt and positively respond to whatever waves come your way. This keeps your attitude as an ally working for you rather than an adversary working against you. You cannot control the waves; you can only control your response to the waves and develop the skills to adapt to whatever comes your way.

The Four Steps of the S.U.R.F. Strategy

S urvey the situation

U nderstand your options

R espond based on your goals

F orward focus in action and attitude

1. **S**urvey the Situation

When you are tumbled by a wave, you have to regain your bearing and figure out exactly where you are. Leave emotion behind and survey your situation. What new opportunities might be found or developed? Now is the opportunity to create a new plan. It might be tempting to get caught up in the heat of the moment and feel like you are without options. Take a step back to gain perspective. With an understanding of where you are and what choices you have, you can make the most of the opportunities.

2. **U**nderstand Your Options

After you know where you are, begin to assess options for moving forward. Focus only on solutions. After you survey your situation, it's time to make way for positive solutions and options. Ask questions like: "What can I gain?" or "What contacts can I make?" Maintain a positive outlook regardless of the situation – even if you do not immediately see the opportunity. Stay focused on the outcome you want and where you want to go.

Look optimistically for creative ways to use the situation for good – don't lament your misfortune. The opportunity may be hidden. Learn to look for it. This is a creative success habit, and it only comes with practice. Become an *opportunity farmer*. Look for the hidden benefits behind each change and every situation.

3. **R**espond Based on Your Goals

Now, assess the options in front of you. Some may be better than others. Some may be more complicated or difficult to see. Weigh the pros and cons of each option. You might find your best option right now is to persist in your current situation. You may find yourself riding a wave bigger than you think you can handle. It may be a terrophoria ride, but at least it will be interesting.

Remember, you always have choices. The only thing you can control is your attitude. Regardless of the wave, you have the power to choose. Make sure your response is in line with your goals.

4. Forward Focus in Action and Attitude

You can't surf yesterday's wave. Think creatively toward the future. Take positive action. Do not let things just happen to you. Create the conditions and outcomes *you* seek! Now that you are surfing the wave, maintain focus on where you want to go and what you want to do. Maintain a vivid mental image of your successful future and find ways to keep taking action in that direction.

Seven Essential Surfing Skills to Revolutionize Your Business and Personal Life

Now that you know the strategy, let's move ahead and look at seven rules for successful surfing – rules you'll soon be living by. The rules you will learn will equip you with skills and techniques to be a great surfer. You already have everything you need. Learn to make the most out of any situation. Equip yourself with the opportunity to surf whatever comes your way. Even when you wipe out, you can still learn, adapt and improve your life.

Prepare your *Carpe Aqualis!* mind-set as you learn to apply the seven essential surfing skills to revolutionize your business and personal life.

- Rule 1: Your competition is not the other surfers; It's only you
- Rule 2: Great surfers strengthen others - *to get promoted, make yourself replaceable*

- <u>Rule 3</u>: Surf the waves that come, but be prepared for the big one!
- <u>Rule 4</u>: Apply No-Wave Thinking
- <u>Rule 5</u>: Be your own "Big Kahuna"
- <u>Rule 6</u>: Surf your passion and your strengths
- <u>Rule 7</u>: Go big or go home! To be great, you have to be willing to wipe out!

As you apply these new understandings and surfing techniques to your life you equip yourself to create a spectacular ride! You will NEVER look at waves and change the same way.

Surf -Titude:

"Carpe Aqualis! is taking personal responsibility to create and nurture the development of opportunities in your life."

Chapter *4*

Rule 1 – Your Competition is Not the Other Surfers; It's Only You

Surf -Titude:

"Success in your career and in your life is NOT you against the world... it is you against you!"

You Don't Have to Out Swim the Shark

Two surfers were lined up waiting for a sweet wave. As they looked toward the horizon, instead of seeing a wave, they saw the horrifying sight of a great white shark, its fin disappearing as it turned toward them. One of the surfers immediately started paddling furiously to the shore. Exasperated with the apparent futility of the situation, the other surfer started to scream, "Dude, are you crazy? You can't outswim a shark; what are you doing?" The surfer on the move replied without even looking back, "I don't have to outswim the shark... I just have to outswim *you!*"

Okay, it's an old joke, but hopefully the point is well taken. Don't focus on the shark and don't focus on the other surfers... focus on the only thing in your control, your ability to get out of danger. Your only real competition is with the face you see in the mirror. Certainly there is competition from others, but you cannot control anyone or anything other than yourself, so why waste energy on it?

Success through Leverage, Value and Partnership

Make no mistake, your success in your career and in life is not you against the world... it is you against you! No matter what you do for a living or who you work for, your long-term security and the level of your reward will depend on your ability to provide leverage, value and partnership to those you serve.

Success is about little things providing a slight advantage over time. These little successes add up to larger successes. You are not competing with others, although you may feel like you are. What others think, say, or do is irrelevant to your situation. Your only competition is with yourself and the self-imposed barriers you desire to break. When you are a surfer sitting in the lineup waiting to take on the wave, it is just between you and the wave. Develop your surfing skills and apply them to your opportunities. Your actions will separate you from the crowd over time. Leverage leads to value, which builds the basis for partnership.

Elevate within the Stewardship Pyramid™

Stewardship is a word not often heard in business circles. It means taking care of the resources entrusted to you and utilizing them as if you were the "owner" of the task, project, or company. It is vital to see yourself as an owner, no matter where you are or for whom you work. This ownership can be translated as, "Please don't worry about me; I own this, so you can focus your attention somewhere else." As you rise in an organization, your level of responsibility and your resulting compensation are based on the ability to master this principle. The Stewardship Pyramid™ is comprised of three layers:

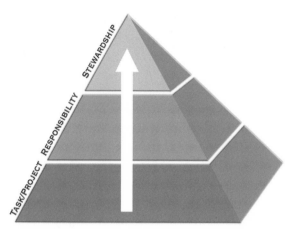

Each layer builds on the other to achieve maximum results and efficiency.

1. **Task/Project** –This level requires a singular focus on an objective – a job or to-do list. At this level, you are responsible for yourself. Tasks coordinated together with a single focus build to the project level. As this process builds it expands the "job" through coordination of multiple tasks and projects. You must not only perform and understand the job and issues, but you also need to have some vision beyond what is at hand.

2. **Responsibility** – This level involves the utilization of resources to ensure that specific goals and objectives are accomplished. It is a management level requiring the coordination of task/project issues and opportunities along with other resources and areas of the business. The responsibility level requires a focus outside of just "the job." The focus is on the overall picture and the desired outcome.

3. **Stewardship** – This is the highest level and transcends your job and/or business unit. It is about "personal ownership" relating to and affecting others. A *steward* is the captain of the ship and the one ultimately responsible for reaching that goal – without excuse and without

fail! If adverse conditions or roadblocks exist, the steward must take responsibility for overcoming them. Remember, you are the only one on your surfboard – *Your world. Your wave.*

Each level of the pyramid is a vital component in the entire structure. It is not possible to arrive at the stewardship level without mastering and understanding the two previous levels. Moving up the pyramid does not negate the foundation below. Quite the contrary, you can achieve stewardship in a task/project level position. You can also be at a responsibility level within a task or project. You can also get grounded in task-level duties when you are the steward.

The Stewardship Pyramid is more than a job classification. *Stewardship can be attained at any level in the pyramid.* Imagine a task/project-level restaurant worker, who is not only doing his own task/project level duties, but who is also acting at the highest capacity (the stewardship level) for that position. He does his job, trains others, contributes more than asked, demonstrates initiative, generates ideas and is fully engaged in the business. This person would be someone to train, develop and give additional responsibilities with an eye toward promotion. Stewardship is not just the destination; it is also how well you manage the journey.

Stewardship is about meeting deadlines and producing the desired results regardless of circumstances, roadblocks or even job descriptions. The "not my job" attitude stalls many people who never realize the self-sabotage that type of outlook brings. Elevate yourself in your organization. The higher you elevate yourself on the pyramid, the more freedom, opportunities and money you will find. Not only that, it is much less crowded. Recognize, learn and master the Stewardship Pyramid and your success will be assured. No matter what level you are currently surfing, act as a steward. Remember the definition of steward is one *entrusted* with resources and responsibility as if they were the owner. How do you measure up?

The Principle of Leverage → Value → Partnership

Leverage, value and partnership are components which coordinate perfectly within the Stewardship Pyramid. They are equal and similar, yet unique. Leverage, value and partnership give muscle and motion to the skeleton of the pyramid. Successful surfers take personal responsibility to coordinate their actions and focus to maximize opportunity in service and significance to others.

Partnership	=	(Stewardship)
Value	=	(Responsibility)
Leverage	=	(Task/Project)

Leverage

Leverage is a commodity. It is a tradeoff of value for value. Employees trade time, effort and activity. Employers trade money, opportunity and other benefits. Leverage alone does not create job security, as employees can easily trade jobs and employers can easily trade employees. Have you ever experienced a situation where some employees work just hard enough not to get fired or some employers provide just enough for people not to quit?

Leverage is simply added advantage. In the physical world, a lever is created by placing a firm object over a fulcrum (an immovable or stationary point) to create a force greater than the original force applied. Think of a seesaw on a playground. Archimedes, the Greek scientist and mathematician, studied the mechanical nature and mathematical advantage of the lever and said, "Give me a lever long enough and a fulcrum on which to place it, and I shall move the world." Leverage allows you to do more with less. My Dad used to remind me, "Remember, big doors move on small hinges!"

Creating leverage through people can be positive or negative, depending on your intent and application. Creating jobs and opportunities for others as they help you drive your business objective forward is positive. Sweatshops and child labor? Negative. When friendships, marriages, partnerships, teams and other relationships work in harmony, leverage is usually present. Leverage allows people to play to their strengths and to provide value to each other.

Keep in mind, leverage is a commodity. If you are only trading your time for a paycheck, you are a commodity and replaceable. In your career, if all you provide is leverage, as soon as that is no longer needed, you are vulnerable. Can you say, "outsource?" Leverage is vital in business and life applications, but it is only the beginning. The next level is a move into value.

Value

Gasoline prices are pretty much the same everywhere. So why do you stop at one gas station over another? Is it the convenience products? Is it the lighting and feeling of safety and security? Is it the food or the ATM or clean restrooms? These factors all add value beyond the commodity dispensed at the pump. If there are only two stations in town with the same price at the pump, your choice will usually follow the value.

Employees and businesses that provide benefits over what is expected are perceived as being valuable. The value might be things like initiative, great attitude, the ability to work without supervision, extra effort, strong relationships with coworkers, the ability to train others, and so on. What do you do at work that makes your job more than a commodity? What do you do that separates and differentiates you from others?

Partnership

Let's go back to our gas station analogy. In trading money for gasoline, we have leverage. Value distinctions play a part in our decision. Now, assume all the gas stations in your area offer roughly the same value. What if one of the stores regularly supports the community with car wash fundraisers, provides a website with information and coupons, or sends you discounts based on what you purchase? They are going to the next level. They are partnering.

Here's a personal example. I am an early morning person. I routinely work out then eat breakfast at a restaurant, spending a couple of quality hours working on projects before the normal distractions of the office intrude. I have dozens of quality restaurant choices (leverage) and have frequented most of them. Restaurants where I get good service, appealing menu choices and a clean atmosphere rise to the value level for me.

One particular Denny's® moved into the partnership category for me, and I now eat there approximately twenty mornings per month. Two of the regular servers, Maria and Pat, take care of me like family. They know my name, know what I regularly order, provide creative menu options consistent with my low-carb diet, bring me the morning newspaper if there is an extra one left, make certain my coffee is never cold and always full. They ensure others provide me with the same level of service. When I am loaded with work, they provide me with extra space. Maria and Pat are definitely part of my business team. They are my partners. That's why I choose their restaurant over so many others.

Partnership happens in surfing as well. Big waves in places like Hawaii and Australia are routinely twenty to thirty feet high. Wiping out in this situation could be a death sentence. Partnership occurs when two partners on a jet ski race in and pull endangered surfers clear before they can be crushed by the force of a giant wave. With each other's lives in the balance, these extreme surfers have no room for a bad day at the office.

Surfing the L.V.P. Wave

How does climbing to the top level of L.V.P. benefit you? Ultimately, "partner" employees are the first ones picked to stay if there are cutbacks. They are the first picked for new opportunities. You can show partnership at any level - from the receptionist to the senior executives. By the same token, longtime executives might offer nothing more than leverage, and they may be lulled into complacency by their tenure and title. What do you think their future holds?

Such corporate politicians, bureaucrats and controllers can actually diminish value or create negative partnerships, where productivity is hindered. Know this: you are owed nothing. The higher you move up in an organization, the more leverage, value and partnership you are expected to demonstrate. As a leader, your success comes through the victories of those you lead.

How do you think your supervisor views you? How would you rate yourself? How do you rate your coworkers and your boss? If you are a supervisor, how would your team rate you?

If you want to grow in your job, figure out how to move from leverage to value to partnership. If you want to earn more money and have more responsibility, then create a plan and take action to move yourself up the L.V.P. scale within the Stewardship Pyramid.

Leverage-only employees are valuable and appreciated only as long as the economic reality stays in their favor. When situations change, they are expendable. Value employees offer leverage plus. Partner employees not only offer value, but they go to the next level. They are "I own this mission" people and are priceless to an organization.

Put yourself in the shoes of a business owner. You took the risk and did all of the initial work to start a business. Everything you have is in this business, and you can only hire so many employees to carry out your vision. What kind of employee would you be looking for?

Promote Yourself! Become the L.V.P. of Your Team

MVP of course stands for Most Valuable Player. Become a Leverage Value Partner employee if you want to promote yourself. Look for opportunities to demonstrate L.V.P. wherever you can.

You may find L.V.P. in long, hard, late hours at work, but that is not necessarily the key. Sometimes that is just window dressing covering up inefficiency. L.V.P. is not difficult to achieve since leverage, value and partnership are provided in the very actions of providing leverage, value and partnership to others. To get paid more, provide more. Do more than you are paid for or you will never earn much more than you are making now. Increase your value and you will be rewarded with increased value. Become a partner to those you serve and you will find partnership coming back to you in other areas.

This is the law of the harvest – sowing and reaping. It is the law of cause and effect. If you are not happy with your results (output), you must look first at the input of value. Rewards come in proportion to service or value rendered. Look for opportunities to exceed the expectations of others and eventually your success will exceed even your own expectations. Be a positive agent for change. Adapt to new opportunities that will come your way.

It is frustrating to watch a person with potential who will not do more until they make more. Have you seen people with this entitlement attitude who feel that showing up or just doing their job entitles them to a raise of income and responsibility? You do not rise through an organization or get true rewards unless you demonstrate your efforts and prove your worth.

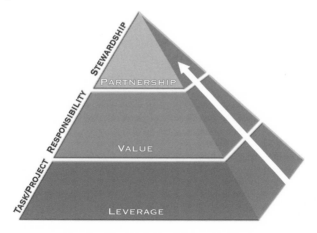

Surf -Titude:

"Unfortunately, average people develop arrogance as they ascend the Stewardship Pyramid, which is completely contrary to partnership. Develop humility and a realization that, although you alone are responsible for you, no one ever climbs to the top alone."

Chapter 5

Rule 2 – Great Surfers Strengthen Others – To Get Promoted, Make Yourself Replaceable

Surf -Titude:

"Don't look at your peers as competition. Learn from them and help them be better surfers. This will enhance your skills and opportunities. Surfing with the best makes you a better surfer."

Have you ever worked with someone who hoarded knowledge as a way to make themselves indispensable? This is pure insecurity at work. People like this don't believe they can stand on their merits, so they try to make themselves impossible to fire. "What would the company possibly do without me? It would fall apart and lose money, because no one knows what I know, or exactly how I do what I do. I'm bulletproof."

Ridiculous! Nobody's indispensable. You might be a miracle worker with knowledge no one could ever hope to duplicate. You might have some mighty big shoes that would be tough for anyone else to fill. Go ahead, gloat. Now think about this: if you are so indispensable your employer can't afford to fire you, how can they ever afford to promote you?

A *controller* is someone who has a commodity (time, expertise, money, authority, and so on) and rations it out in a way that makes others dependent on them. A controller could be a CEO, an accountant, the computer guy or even a secretary. You know what I mean if you've ever worked with one, because you dread asking them for anything. It would be easier to break into Fort Knox than to get any meaningful assistance from them. They might reluctantly assist you but on their terms and conditions. They never let you forget how much you need them. Whether the control factor is handing out paychecks, gaining access to resources or getting a frozen computer running again, it's all about power. It's about being indispensable.

But here's the truth: controllers are always replaceable, and they're usually replaced quickly. Their security is false. What they have is not true security; it's corporate extortion.

Surfers familiar with a geographic area have knowledge about the waves and the best places to line up to catch one. But controller surfers won't share information. They will just watch you get pummeled until you figure it out for yourself. They think that since they had to learn the hard way, so should you. Don't do this. Make the path easier for those who follow you. Take pride in the success of others.

Conventional wisdom says to make yourself irreplaceable. The Carpe Aqualis! philosophy is to "be replaceable." Pass on what you know and help others become better and more capable. As you equip others for success, you will see positive results for yourself. True leaders inspire others to improve and make it easier for them to do so. Add value to everyone you work with, regardless of level, position or immediate value to you. It is a great way to live your life, and the law of reciprocity will repay you.

Stop looking at others as competition. When you strengthen others, you strengthen yourself. In the end, that delivers value to the organization. If you hard-wired yourself into a position where they cannot do without you, how can they possibly consider losing you to a promotion? Instead, look for ways to teach others and assist in their growth. Teach people to replace you. Then you can move up when they take your place. Do not let fear of someone replacing you stop you from adding the most value to your teammates. Don't control, *contribute!*

Don't Be a Crab

Put crabs in a bucket and they're complacent until one tries to climb out. Then the others will pull the would-be jail breaker back down into the bucket. Sometimes we want company in our misery. We let our pride blind us to the fact that if the team wins, we all win. If the crabs just cooperated, they could easily escape. Instead, they bicker and no one gets anywhere. Eventually, they become either dinner or bait.

People often view the success of others as their own failures. Rather than feeling left behind, these corporate crabs hoard ideas, information, and insights that might be valuable to others or to the company. Why help someone else survive or even advance in a culture where information and ideas can be used to wield power? These jealous, insecure people listen to their pride, putting their own selfish needs ahead of those of their colleagues or of their employer. They do not realize that if they help others excel, they will improve their company's fortunes and their own (a rising ride lifts all surfboards). It's a small-minded, petty way to be.

Ironically, this behavior ultimately holds them back from reaching their own goals. After all, when the bucket gets shaken, dynamics change, and suddenly they are dependent on the goodwill and generosity of others, corporate crabs don't get a lot of sympathy.

Surfing our global economy means seeing colleagues not as rivals but as allies. Leaders who actually live teamwork see the benefits of shared creativity and productivity. People who look to gain an advantage by holding back the progress of others might have their day, but they will never have long-term success.

Most People are Not Surfers; They are Posers (Status-Quo Surfer Wannabees)

There are no shortcuts on the path to demonstrating value to others. Words mean nothing; value must be demonstrated. Sometimes this means coming in early and staying late. It means pushing yourself beyond what you thought were your limits. It means finding ways to do things better and more efficiently. It means leverage, value and partnership to the team and the goals of the team. When you live this, what employer would not be excited about you being on the team?

Your goal should be to make yourself indispensable as a leader, as a catalyst of success for the whole team around you. The greater your success and the higher you rise, the more humble you need to be. The more you achieve success, the more you need to recognize and appreciate the support of those who make it possible. Achieve your victories through the victories of others. The best part? You never have to watch your back.

Surf -Titude:

"Let the success of those you serve be the fuel for your success and your ultimate measurement of it."

Chapter 6

Rule 3 – Surf the Waves that Come, but Be Prepared for the Big One!

Surf -Titude:

"In life, there are really only waves of challenges and opportunities. Both have the power to wipe you out or give you a tremendous ride. The only difference is in your approach."

Make Change Work for You

Daydream with purpose. Allow the plan of your life to unfold. Most people do not live their life with purpose, nor do they live their life *on* purpose. One day turns into the next with only weekends and a few holidays to break up the routine. One day spins into another, becoming a week, then a month, then a year. Before you know it, you're locked on a path you never intended to follow and twenty years have passed. You find yourself on a paycheck-to-paycheck path with no end in sight.

Waves Represent Chaos... They Also Represent Opportunity

Deep into the twentieth century and for all of history before it, time moved at crock-pot speed. Now early in the twenty-first century, we are moving at microwave speed and it continues to accelerate. The availability of new information mixed with the speed of processing combined with rapid communication all feed and build on each other. This further builds and intensifies the waves of change in a perfect storm-like convergence. We used to be able to sip and savor information. In our hyper-information age, we are drinking from a fire hydrant.

From the early 1900s until now, you can see the tremendous waves of change forever destroying the previous landscape. The horse and buggy industry passed away with the birth of the automobile and Henry Ford's assembly-line process to make cars for the masses. The automotive industry has adapted and grown through tremendous innovation and change in the last one hundred years. Imagine what the next hundred will bring!

Thomas Alva Edison invented the phonograph in 1877. The first medium for recordings was cylindrical. The sound was audible but scratchy and hollow. From there we went to thick vinyl records and a turntable cranked by hand. This turned into three-speed turntables for the three sizes of records. This progressed into eight-track tapes then reel-to-reel recording for the sophisticated sound system. Next came regular cassette tapes, high capacity tapes, which then moved aside for CDs. We now have MP3s and devices like the IPOD® with new technology giving birth to even better storage options and higher quality formats.

If you do not like change, imagine what it was like for the top executives in any of the industries made obsolete by the new technology. Opportunity is born out of change. New technology and new industries are created out of the ashes of what has come before.

Chaos or Opportunity? It's All in Your Perspective

It takes a bit of perspective to see change as good and useful. Forest fires are destructive and pose a significant risk for loss of life and property, but they're necessary as part of nature's cycle to rejuvenate itself. When a wooded area gets overgrown and has lots of dead underbrush, a fire clears it. The ashes replenish the soil and promote new growth.

Outsourcing is a force in business today, for good or ill, depending on your perspective. It's been tremendous for the temporary help industry and for niche businesses designed to do one thing better than anyone else. If however, you have a job outsourced to another company or country, it is somewhat difficult for you to see the up side.

My friend Mary has had four different jobs with four different titles and four different business cards, yet she only accepted one job offer, has not quit and has not been fired. Richard, a former bank president friend of mine, worked for three different banks with three different business cards without ever quitting or being fired. I know several others in industries as varied as convenient store chains and radio stations, who have worked for three or more different companies without ever being fired or quitting. How is this possible? If you have not already guessed, it is because of mergers and acquisitions. Business changes daily, sometimes hourly. This forced change, like most waves, brings both chaos and opportunity.

My father worked as a salesperson for the same company for more than fifteen years. They were locked in a bitter rivalry with a large competitor – who later acquired his company. I will never forget one day at the breakfast table, watching him stare at his new business card with his name under the logo of his arch enemy. It was sobering to watch my dad adjust to his new reality. Is the change in your life chaos or opportunity? It all depends on your perspective.

The Judo of Situation Transformation

What do judo and surfing have in common? Both use the force and momentum of the adversary to their advantage. Judo (Japanese for "the gentle way") is the martial art of redirecting force. The basic premise is to use the force and momentum of your attackers against them. When they throw a punch or lunge at you, they have taken themselves off center and presented you with an advantage. If you have the skill, you can redirect their size and strength to your advantage with a throw or a take down. Judo is thousands of years old and has a tradition of allowing smaller opponents to win over larger and stronger foes.

Surfing is exactly the same. The wave is vastly more powerful than you, but with training and practice, you can learn to use its force and energy to your advantage. In your life and career, you should be doing the same thing, using the art of *situation transformation*. This skill and mind-set allows you to take situations others may classify as bad or negative, redirect the force and energy to your benefit and turn the situation to your advantage.

For example, imagine you are laid off in a downsizing move. You have a choice: you can look at this as a negative and be depressed or you can turn it into an opportunity. If you practice situation transformation, the layoff becomes a challenge. It may be a call to start your own business using the skills and contact network you've built on the job, or it may be a chance to go back to school for a different career. With the right frame of mind, chaos becomes opportunity.

This does not come easily at first. We are conditioned to see uncertainty as frightening, something to be avoided. It can be, but not if you redirect its energy. Rather than escape, think about leveraging the situation. This is the time to imagine. What could you do? Where could this lead you? What can you learn?

Entrepreneurship is about seeing what everyone else sees, then thinking originally and creatively. It is about relating the normally unrelated. Newton observed an apple fall from a tree and thought about gravity. Benjamin Franklin observed lightning and ended up harnessing electricity for hundreds of inventions that we use today. Nearly every great discovery began with an observer relating the normally unrelated.

Make the Most of the Waves You Encounter

How you handle difficulty and hardship reveals your character. Adversity faced makes us stronger. It's like carrying a weight around willingly. Your muscles grow and become more powerful. So does your character. The mere act of accepting adversity with a positive attitude and a proactive approach makes you more able to overcome it. As Thomas Paine wrote, "The harder the conflict, the more glorious the triumph."

We can't control the weather or the waves. The same surf will make some people joyous and others miserable. The ocean in itself is neither good nor bad. Some days will bring good surf. Others bring storms. Often storms bring the best surf. How you weather a storm is your choice. That choice will leave you stronger and more resolute or weaker and discouraged.

Adversity is an unforgiving revealer of character. The good news is, if you don't like what adversity shows you, you can change it. Character isn't static. Challenge and adversity allow you the opportunity to choose your response and your action. You can change your character and grow into the person you wish to become by taking full advantage of the adversity in your life. Learn and grow in each difficulty and you will be better prepared for anything that comes your way.

Carpe Aqualis! Make the Most of the Waves You are Given!

Make sure the waves you are surfing and the actions you are taking move toward your major goal. Do not move from wave to wave unfocused on your goal. Do not fall short of your objectives because of a lack of focus. Change will happen as a recurring theme in your life. Do not just deal with change; harness it and use it as a force for good in your life and in your career.

Carpe Aqualis! as an identity creates a results-oriented problem solver. It is an adaptation skill to take what is given to you and adapt to it. Do not just survive change; thrive on it as you surf the waves you are given. When you surf the waves in front of you, you build your skills and proficiencies to better prepare for the great waves that will come later. You have to be in position, making the most of where you are today if you want to take on the big waves of tomorrow.

Learn How to Duck Dive

Most people do not ever get into the proper position for surfing because they approach the waves tentatively. As they meekly paddle out, incoming waves crest and break on top of them, pushing them back. A few attempts and they quit. They never get past the zone where the surf breaks and never get the chance to really surf and master a big wave.

In real surfing, there are several techniques to get through the crashing waves. One is called "duck diving." When paddling out to get into the line up, a surfer will grab the side edges or "rails" of the board and dive directly into an oncoming wave. This allows the surfer to cut through the wave without getting pushed backward and losing all progress.

In your own confrontations with change and adversity, the duck dive can come in handy. Using it, you'll face your waves squarely. You'll attack them instead of being on the defensive. It may not be pretty, but it is effective. The larger the waves are that you attack and the more frequently you attack them, the more you will improve in this essential skill.

Always Be Prepared for the Big One!

You will never know when the next great opportunity will come, where it will come from or what it will be. You have no control over the weather, global trade, macro-economic trends, value of currencies, geo-politics or anything else. The only thing you can control is your response, skills, abilities and attitude. Stay prepared and ready. Observe the trends, tendencies and actions of the waves on your beach. Preparing yourself for the big one will not go unrewarded.

Nobody can surf your wave but you. It would be nice to delegate our life results to someone else, but this will not happen. No one will do it for you, nor could anyone even if they wanted to. Your parents cannot. Your spouse cannot. Your boss, friend, minister, therapist or children cannot.

Learn to reset your thermostat to change your environment rather than just reflect the environment like a thermometer. You are the only one who has the leverage to take control and to affect your outcomes. There is no one who can be a better advocate for you than you.

Surf -Titude:

"The more difficult the wave, the more spectacular the ride!"

Chapter 7

Rule 4 – Apply No-Wave Thinking™

Surf-Titude:

"In good times, enjoy. In difficult times, grow."

If You Miss a Wave, Another Will Come

Surfing the waves you are given allows you to learn, adapt and grow. Opportunity is meaningless by itself. It is like telling someone they have "potential." That really means, "You have ability, but you haven't done anything with it yet!" Opportunity is a blank canvas; to turn it into a masterpiece, you've got to work. It's a wave moving toward you, and you're in the right position. Many people find opportunities, yet they fail to realize their potential. The swell lifts them momentarily, but they fail to catch the wave. The other side of the swell lets them down as the water reaches its lowest point before rising to normal levels again. If you let it pass you by, it's meaningless. Some people will sit on their board all day and yet never catch a wave.

Don't Ride a Bad Wave All the Way

No-Wave Thinking™ is a strategy you should use to evaluate all opportunities. Ask yourself, "Knowing what I know now, would I still ride this wave?" If the answer is no, with no sound reason to stay with it, bail out. If the answer is yes, ride it as long and as far as you can. Apply No-Wave Thinking to every area of your life. Ask yourself whether there is anything you are doing, knowing what you now know, you would not continue to do today. If you find something, change it. Otherwise, you're staying with a bad wave.

Remember, you can only ride one wave at a time. If you choose to stay on one, you cannot ride a different one without abandoning the first one. If you choose to abandon a wave, you've got to be committed to the new one, because once the old wave is gone, it's gone.

This isn't a call to immediately quit your job or a relationship, as these relationships are certainly more complicated than this simple metaphor. However, you should evaluate where you are and apply No-Wave Thinking. If something is not working, at least take action to understand and improve where you are. You are not doing your relationship, yourself or your organization any favors if you cannot give your all. If you find yourself over your head on your wave, there is nothing wrong with jumping off and starting again. It is certainly more graceful than losing your shorts on a wipe out!

When Bad Surf Happens to Good Surfers

As you surf life's waves, you will see good waves and bad ones. You will have some awesome rides and some gnarly wipe outs. You will meet fellow surfers who want to help you out and those who would rather beat you down. There will be sunny days to enjoy the beach. There will also be storms that take away your enjoyment and opportunity as the sea becomes unstable and unsuitable for your purposes. Injustice, rude people, hardships, difficulties and even some bad things will happen in your life. We cannot control those. The only thing we can control is our attitude and the actions we choose to take in response.

Living is not about playing it safe. Test yourself. Learn the full measure of your surfing ability. Do not hide from the waves. You can learn from both your great rides and your wipe outs.

Opportunity does not come to the passive. Be active and create your opportunities. Sometimes opportunities come only through difficult situations. *Adversity doesn't build character, it reveals it.* How you choose to respond to adversity reveals your true character. Your true character is uncovered in the actions of your response and in the choices you make. Your character is revealed in the promises you keep and in the convictions you hold true. Ultimately, your character is a mirror of the guiding principles in your life. What you do and say reveal to the world who you are.

Look for Blessings in Adversity™

I believe in the power of prayer and have prayed for many things in my life. I feel some have been answered directly while others have been answered in a different way. Looking back, some of the very best things that have ever happened to me came as the result of prayers that seemed to go unanswered. Life events that I once saw as heartache and disappointment later became opportunities and blessings. If I had been spared the experience of those tough times, I would not have the family, business, opportunities and friendships I enjoy today.

Even in my son Frankie's experience with leukemia, we discovered blessings beyond belief. Our involvement with St. Jude Children's Research Hospital dramatically changed my focus as an author and entrepreneur. Our limited scope of observation and the typical human short-term view does not always allow for the full perspective on the new opportunities to be found in difficulties and adversities.

When bad surf happens to good surfers, it's their response that determines the outcome. It does not help to be angry at the waves. We discussed the S.U.R.F Strategy as a response to the waves of change in your life. When difficult and unexpected situations arise, this response is even more important. It's critical to learn to cultivate potential blessings and opportunities in your adversities. There is no guarantee they will be there, but you won't know unless you learn how to look.

Applying the S.U.R.F. Strategy in Difficulties and Adversities

1. **S**urvey the Situation
After the storm is over, survey the damage and create a new plan.

2. **U**nderstand Your Options
Assess options for moving forward. Discuss solutions rather than problems. Resolve to maintain a positive outlook regardless of the situation. Stay solution-based, with your focus on looking for ways of using the situation for good rather than to lament about your misfortune.

Without resistance, there can be no growth. Most people don't lift weights for the joy of it; they challenge themselves with growing resistance to get stronger.

Look for hidden gifts. You will never know when an obstacle is hiding an opportunity. But if you don't look, you'll never find it. Develop the mind-set that the challenge you are facing has been specifically given to you to help you learn, develop and grow. Look for the hidden potential benefits. At the very least, see if you can learn a lesson to apply to the future.

3. **R**espond Based on Your Goals
With several options available to you, apply your creativity to ensure your response is in line with your goals.

Do not react to what happens to you; respond instead with a plan of action. Come up with a creative, positive plan of action that leads to a specific goal. Then get moving.

4. Forward Focus Your Action and Attitude

Focus on the future rather than on the past. Do not waste emotional energy on worry or blame. Maintain your focus on where you want to go and what you want to do.

Assume you invested one thousand dollars into a dot com start up, which is now worth $250. What are your options? You could moan about your loss. You could vow never to invest and keep your money in your mattress. You could choose to throw more money at it, figuring it would not be fair for this stock not to go back up and make you whole. Or you could survey, understand and respond, and then forward focus on options in line with your investment goals. The S.U.R.F. Strategy keeps you moving toward your objectives, converting challenges into opportunities that improve your surfing skills for today and tomorrow.

Yesterday's Wave is Long Gone

You cannot change what happened yesterday. Instead, find the lesson and use it to benefit your tomorrow. Don't punish yourself with regrets. Do not hold the past so close that it prevents your future. Whatever you have gone through, whatever your previous circumstances, it's done. You can choose to learn from it or not. As always, it's your choice.

Learn from your past, but focus on the future. With a *Carpe Aqualis!* mind-set, yesterday's successes and failures are your investments in tomorrow. Don't overcomplicate the process. It really is as simple as one, two, three.

1. Learn from the past.
2. Live in the present.
3. Plan, prepare and take action toward your future.

Surf -Titude:

"Never turn your back on the waves of the ocean. It is far better to see what is coming so that you can respond or adapt than to be blind-sided."

It May Not be Your Fault, But it is Your World and it is Your Wave

You are where you are. Accept it and move forward. You can't surf yesterday's wave. Don't be locked into hurts or issues from your past. This ultimately diminishes today, which also takes away from your future. If you were wronged or hurt in the past, go ahead and scream, "It's not my fault!" Feel better? Good. Now, here's the harsh truth: no one cares. Blame isn't the issue, responsibility is. Self-pity, blame and accusation will not move you forward. No matter what was done *to* you, you are the only one who can take responsibility for today, make smart choices and ride your wave in a way that does great things *for* you.

Once, I was watching my son playing outside when he was a toddler. I could see him, but he did not know where I was. He fell down and started crying, waiting for someone to pick him up and comfort him. While I watched and listened, he wailed, until he finally realized that no one was coming to pick him up. Then he stopped crying, got up and kept on playing. Maybe that sounds harsh, but my goal as a parent is to raise a self-reliant, independent son. The lesson is this: no one is coming to pick you up, so stop crying and keep moving.

Discouragement and setbacks happen. Your response will determine the outcome. Use setbacks as excuses to learn and improve. This is called "failing forward." As you become adept at moving through obstacles, you'll get stronger and be more able to achieve your goals.

Surf -Titude:

"Success in surfing is not about the waves in your life but rather your approach to surfing those waves."

Chapter *8*

Rule 5 – Be Your Own "Big Kahuna"

Surf -Titude:

**"Success is found where opportunity
meets personal responsibility."**

Do You Have Twenty Years of Experience or One Year of Experience Repeated Twenty Times?

Longevity in a company or profession isn't enough to make you a guru. You might know people like this. They've been with the company forever. Unfortunately, if they are not changing, adapting, learning and growing, they are on a career treadmill. Quality of time means more than quantity of time.

To be competitive and successful in your career, you've got to grow with time. Use the many books, coaches, courses and resources available to become your own "Big Kahuna."

Becoming Your Own "Big Kahuna"

Kahuna is derived from the Hawaiian title for a shaman and literally means expert, wizard or guru. I believe that everyone can benefit from having a great coach. It's important to have someone to give you honest, candid insight outside of your own biased perspective. Having another point of view can only help you.

However, you should be your own Kahuna. The word *guru* as part of the Kahuna definition means revered teacher or mentor and recognized leader. It also has come to represent a kind of hero worship and idolatry. Find a coach or mentor whose teachings you respect, but never let anyone become your guru. It robs you of control. Take counsel and coaching from others, but you can never forget the lesson of personal responsibility: Your World. Your Wave.

To Thine Own Self be True... Become Your Own Guru

As you learn, grow, and adapt to your waves, you can develop the skill to become your own success coach. There are thousands of success coaches and books. You could waste hundreds of thousands of dollars looking to someone else to tell you how to live your life and succeed. Not only is this not necessary, but it's ineffective. No one else can choose how you respond to your wave.

You have both the ability and the responsibility to be your primary success coach. Keep it simple. No matter what your goals are, there are only four basic questions you need to be able to answer.

1. **Where are you now?**
2. **Why are you where you are?**
3. **Where do you want to go?**
4. **How will you get there?**

Before reading any further, take a moment to answer these questions utilizing your new Carpe Aqualis! mind-set.

Bombard Your Brain with New Ideas and Information

You can achieve amazing things when you flood your mind with new information. Read everything you can, talk to people who have done what you want to do, explore all avenues. Listen to others and remain open to all ideas, but ultimately be your own Kahuna and make your own decisions. You can take advice from others, but that will never take away your responsibility. Your doctor is not responsible for your health, your accountant is not responsible for your taxes, and your mechanic is not responsible for the upkeep of your car. They are valued parts of your team, but they offer only guidance and counsel. The responsibility is always yours.

How to be a Visionary in One Easy Lesson

Would you like to know some secret, never-before-revealed techniques to tell the future and become a visionary? Well, I cannot help you with the lottery, sports betting or where you lost your car keys, but I can teach you how to employ tools used by great leaders throughout history to interpret the future.

There was a special on FOX several years back where they revealed the secrets of magicians, causing a great uproar. They took away the mystique and mystery behind magic's most treasured secrets making it look easy. Being a *visionary* (someone who sees potential in new ideas and how they can become a reality) is similar in the appearance of mystique and mystery. In reality, it is a skill you can learn and apply to your life. There are eight tools available to create and foretell your compelling vision of the future. The more you employ the more effective your visioning skills will be. Below are the components of what I call the Vision 88 toolkit (so-called because each of the eight words ends in "ate").

1. **Create**
2. **Elevate**
3. **Triangulate**
4. **Extrapolate**
5. **Interpolate**
6. **Educate**
7. **Communicate**
8. **Reframiate** (Okay, I made this one up to maintain the pattern.)

Use individually and combine for more power to vision-cast like the pros. Utilizing these tools, you'll have the amazing power to predict what your life or career will look like in the future and actually make it happen.

Create

Pick a number between one and ten. Now guess your number. Did you get it right? Isn't that cool? The best possible way to see the future is to envision it then create it. Do not look past the power you hold to create your future. There will be things outside your control that can take you off course, but you have the power to steer around them.

Here's the rub. If you do not create your own future, you will be at the mercy of someone else's vision of your future. Then your future is literally accidental. It's hard to be a success by accident.

In our office, we have ten values clearly posted for everyone to read. The concluding and summarizing value is: "We are excited about our business opportunities, knowing... *the best way to predict the future is to create it!*" Be the architect and create your vision of the future then take action to make it happen.

Elevate

Rise above a problem to gain a different perspective. I live in a small town about twenty minutes' drive from my office. When I drive in every day, I have one perspective. My part of Illinois is flat farmland, but I can't see my destination.

But when I fly, I get a completely different vantage point. I can see my path as well as alternate paths. As a bonus, I can see beyond my goal to other places I might go.

Nearly everyone who comes to me with problems has blinded himself or herself to the view of opportunities and solutions. They hold their problems and worries too close. This is like writing your problem on a piece of paper then holding it so close to your face that you can't read it. To change your perspective on a situation, step back a little to get a different viewpoint.

Stand on the beach and watch the waves before you paddle out. You'll see how they break, where they grow tallest, and where the opportunities are. A different perspective improves your ride.

Triangulate

When I was learning land navigation and survival skills in the Army, we used triangulation to figure where we were by using two known and visible reference points. Assume you are standing on a football field. If you had a map and a compass then drew two lines on the map from the two goal posts to where you stood, where the two lines crossed would be your location on the map. Surveyors use this tool every day, as do pilots and boat captains.

Triangulation is an effective tool to figure out the best route to take toward your destination. Surfers use this technique, using two different points on the shore to find the ideal spot to catch good waves. Sometimes you'll get to your goal fastest by going in a straight line; other times, you're better off going at an angle.

Creative people surf ideas and triangulate information, ideas and even relationships. Their minds are fluid and adaptable as well as flexible enough to challenge status quo, straight-line thinking. Creative people are non-linear thinkers, sometimes going from point A to point B but making stops at point L and point Q along the way.

If you keep yourself educated and knowledgeable, you'll be able to make connections beyond the immediate scope of the situation. Genius is not necessarily creating new idea, but seeing how existing ideas can be used in new ways to address a situation.

Learn to relate what is normally unrelated. Practice looking for patterns and relationships in things you would not normally associate. Jesus used parables to make complicated concepts simple. Aesop told fables to help people understand. As you train your mind, unrelated information and knowledge will lead to new insights. Some of the biggest business successes were adaptations of unrelated ideas. Nurture your desire for knowledge.

Extrapolate

To extrapolate is to discern unknown information by building on what you already know. As you analyze the known information and carry it forward, you can predict future results. If you draw a line from point A to point B and then continue the line to guess where point C will be along the same line, you're extrapolating.

If you are trying to lose twenty pounds and are currently losing two pounds per week, you can extrapolate that in ten weeks, you'll be able to celebrate. It's predicting the future not based on tarot cards or a crystal ball but on real data.

One definition of insanity is doing the same thing and expecting different results. If you continue along your current path, your results will be the same as in the past. If you change your path, your results will be different. If you want to create a different future, create a new path and begin to act differently. Learn from where you are and look forward with a new vision of where you want to be.

Interpolate

As extrapolate means to project the future with current information, interpolate means to take what is known and look inward. It's a tool used in math to estimate or determine a value between two or more known values. Knowing 2, 4, 8, ??, 32, we can interpolate the missing number as 16.

Take what you know and look inward. Determine what might be missing or what should be added. If you have a jigsaw puzzle with a recognizable picture all put together with the exception of a couple of pieces, your mind would naturally interpolate to fill in the blanks in the picture. Use this vision skill to fill in the blanks. Based on your goals and your projected future, what skills or knowledge do you need?

Educate

Embrace your ignorance. To get smart you have to be willing to be ignorant. You have to realize how much you *don't* know so you know what you need to learn. Become an insatiable seeker of knowledge. Read everything you can get your hands on. Educate yourself, learn your industry, know your company, discover trends. Learn to love discovering new information.

Communicate

What good is a vision if you don't share it? Communicating your vision to others is essential if you want to attract collaborators or inspire others to help you. Share your vision with others – passionately, specifically, confidently. To create a vision and see the future, you need to see it in your mind first. To describe it to others, you need to use descriptive word pictures and colorful and descriptive adjectives to convey the emotion and passion the words are meant to represent. "I see it; let me share my vision with you, so you can believe it!"

Refram(iat)e

Reframing a situation is taking a look at a situation from a different perspective, or looking for new outcomes. Many times we get trapped into linear thinking and fix our minds on a certain outcome. Although it is difficult to see at the time, disappointments often benefit us. Could you imagine having married the first person you thought you were in love with? By reframing, we re-assess the opportunities that might come from an unexpected outcome.

Your ability to reframe what other people see as difficult situations and turn them around with a positive attitude will quickly separate you from your peer group. Others may call it luck, but as a life entrepreneur, you know the power of perspective allows you to stack the cards in your favor.

To Find Enlightenment You Must First Embrace Ignorance

The path to enlightenment begins with ignorance! Embrace your inner ignorance. You may have never heard anyone embrace ignorance before, but true enlightenment is actually building your positive ignorance. Let me explain. Ignorance is darkness found in what you do not know. Enlightenment is having the light turned on to take away the darkness of ignorance.

One of the greatest assets you possess is curiosity. Channel it and challenge it. Do not be held back by ignorance. Learn to embrace it and use it as a tool. The secret to genius is learning to master the art of ignorance. Contemplate this concept for a moment.

When you are fully committed and begin the journey of learning, you will become far more ignorant than before you began your quest. To get smart you have to be willing to be ignorant as a path to growth through failure and then understanding. Before you can truly become smart, you have to realize, accept and embrace how much you do not know. As you begin to know what you don't know, you can take action so that you will know.

This is a positive cycle of expanding your ignorance to get smarter. This may take a minute to wrap your brain around, but to expand your knowledge, you must be willing to intelligently expand your ignorance first. Developing your ignorance creates a vacuum for knowledge to replace the void created.

1. What you know you know (knowledge)
2. What you know you don't know (intelligent ignorance)
3. What you don't know you don't know (blissful ignorance)

Educate. Enlighten. Empower. The path to empowerment consists of E³ – education, enlighten, empower!

* **Education** is information leading to knowledge. What you do with the knowledge shared in this book can just be read and never acted upon or it can be applied.
* **Enlightenment** is positively planned ignorance leading to the acquisition of knowledge through education. It is taking the knowledge shared and understanding, even embracing, how much you don't know. This allows you to start digging in for further understanding and a practical knowledge base that lets you take action.
* **Empowerment** is applied enlightenment. It is knowledge mixed with action. Empowerment literally means to give power. This provides tremendous leverage as you take action on what you *do* know based on what you *did not* know before. Empowerment is about equipping yourself with knowledge powered with action. Many will read this and nod their heads in agreement, yet never change anything in their lives. Ultimately, empowerment is *action wrapped around knowledge and applied to your life with focus.*

Reading a book or watching a video on surfing is knowledge. Knowing two styles and methods of surfing is also knowledge. Realizing there are twenty other techniques and styles you did not know about is enlightenment. Applying that knowledge to the practical application of improving your skills is empowerment.

Henry David Thoreau observed, "To know that we know what we know, and that we do not know what we do not know, that is true knowledge." We are all born into the world ignorant and without knowledge. Whether we choose to remain ignorant or take action to adapt and apply knowledge to our advantage over our environment is a choice. Each choice or series of choices culminates over time in our destiny. The real question is whether we want to end up where fate takes us or take control to whatever degree we can to choose our own destination. Knowledge applied to your life gives you power over your life and leverage to affect your own future.

Surf -Titude:

"Live your life on purpose rather than by default. Design it, build it, live it, enjoy it!"

Chapter 9

Rule 6 – Surf Your Passion and Your Strengths

Surf -Titude:

"Learning to 'seize the wave' will change your situation. Learning to seize 'your' wave will change your life."

The Formula for Achieving Greatness

The formula for success and for greatness is to mix your passion with your purpose and develop your strengths. The formula for average achievement is to work on your weaknesses while your strengths get little attention.

The best basketball player to ever play the game is Michael Jordan. Why? Because his passion for the game led to his habit of challenging himself to improve his already phenomenal skill-set. He is a poster boy for the formula of greatness. When he was praised for his brilliant offensive skills, he took it as a challenge to be the best defensive player. Dominating players inside with breathtaking slam dunks, he was brilliant. Not satisfied, he pushed himself to become a great outside shooter. Every season he played, Jordan built on his strengths, which was fueled by his burning desire.

Could Jordan still have been excellent without pushing himself the way he did? Probably. His natural talents were that astonishing. But the passion and zeal he brought to his game lifted him to heights never before seen. Contrast this with the two years he didn't play basketball to try his hand at major league baseball. Sure, he worked hard and passionately, but he could not play to his natural strengths. As a baseball player, he was a washout. Upon returning to the NBA, he again dominated.

The point is simply to learn to surf your strengths and passions. Learn how to outsource, delegate or to "just say no" where you are weak. This way you can build and develop your strengths. If you don't have a passion for what you are doing, you need to find something else... unless you are satisfied with average. Mix your talents and strengths with enough passion to drive you and it will take an army to hold you back.

Developing an Entrepreneurial Mind-Set

You do not have to start your own business to have an entrepreneurial mind-set. Being an entrepreneur is about taking a new, creative approach to an old situation. You could be a minister, a teacher, a secretary in an office, a sales representative or the head of a large company and have the opportunity to apply creative solutions to a situation to achieve the results you seek. A surfing, entrepreneurial mind-set challenges the status quo. It frees you to look at situations and resources in a different way.

Point Your Board in the Right Direction

If your board is pointed out to sea, you will not be able to surf to the shore. Point your board in the direction you want to go. Positive expectancy is not about overlooking evidence of a negative outcome. It is not viewing the world with rose-colored glasses or being blissfully ignorant. Instead, it is about training yourself to be optimistic about the results you have prepared for. You will still have failures and setbacks as part of learning. Positive expectancy is about believing in yourself and your dreams, even when no one else does. It's about seeing what you want to happen before it even happens.

When you are focused on your desired outcome, you create the conditions to bring it to reality. Fear, worry and doubt become self-fulfilling prophecies.

When the Wave Hits, Take Action and Paddle Like Crazy

When you find the great wave you have been waiting for, it is not enough to let the momentum carry you. Paddle like crazy – take swift, decisive action. Launch new ideas, propose new initiatives or start new projects to create your own momentum.

Just because you are part of a team or a company on the move does not mean anything. If you think anyone is going to carry you to the finish line or bring you with them to the big party just because... you are in for a big disappointment.

When you find yourself in the beginning swell of the wave, paddle like you are trying to beat the wave to shore. When your ride begins as the board moves with the power of the wave, that's the take off. If you don't have enough speed or momentum, you will either miss the wave as the swell races under you or be dumped as the wave crashes over you. The faster you are moving as the wave develops, the better your chance to ride it all the way in.

Believe You are a Surfer to Become One

Before you can become a *Carpe Aqualis!* surfer, you must develop the mind-set of one. Your thoughts determine your life. They are the beginning of all your endeavors. Belief influences your actions. Your belief system is your underlying set of rules – the operating system for how you see, judge, create and live your reality. If you subconsciously believe you are incompetent, you'll never hold a job for long, because your belief thermostat sabotages your efforts. Beliefs control attitudes. Attitudes control emotions. Emotions control actions. When you believe something, you are hardwired to have a result consistent with that belief.

Surf as If

To become the person you want to be, first change how you think. That, in turn, will change your actions. You can create a positive self-fulfilling prophecy by changing your patterns of action. When you can begin to visualize and see yourself as you want to be – when you truly believe you are a surfer of change – you will move closer to your goal.

Harvard psychologist William James observed, "If you want a quality, act as if you already had it." William Shakespeare said, "Assume a virtue, if you have it not." Dale Carnegie remarked, "Act as if you were already happy, and that will tend to make you happy." Belief fueled by desire and commitment strengthens you to paddle your board to where you need to be. Make new decisions about what is possible. Decide that you are not at the mercy of others, circumstances or fate.

You may be in a tough place in your life where you feel you do not have much control, but you do. It is like being in a tight parking space. You need to get out, but you are so blocked in that you only have a few inches. You turn the wheel and move a few inches back. Rotate the wheel the other way and move a few inches to the front. Back and forth, you are only able to move slightly, however each move buys you a little more room than your previous spacing. Each action provides you with more room and more leverage until eventually you are free. Your life is no different.

Program Yourself for Successful Surfing

Look for the good in every situation. This does not mean you should turn into a modern-day Pollyanna or delude yourself into thinking positively while the *Titanic* is sinking beneath you. The lesson is to assess each situation for the opportunities and the benefits that are surely there. This is often difficult due to the emotion clouding the situation. Losing a job is an event that happens to millions of people each year. You could look at this predicament and see only the negative or you could see the opportunities presented.

The Chinese symbol of yin and yang represents the coexistence and the benefit played by problems and opportunities. Former President Richard M. Nixon explained the same type of dichotomy in the Chinese symbol representing the word *crisis*: "The Chinese use two brush strokes to write the word crisis. One brush stroke stands for danger; the other for opportunity. In a crisis, be aware of the danger – but recognize the opportunity."

Learn to recognize opportunity and remain alert for the situations that are able to give birth to success. To do this, it is important to get and maintain a positive attitude. When you practice this attitude, it allows you to see the possibilities when opportunity comes – because it usually shows up disguised as adversity and no one else recognizes it. Winston Churchill observed, "The pessimist sees difficulty in every opportunity. The optimist sees the opportunity in every difficulty."

Surfer Affirmations

When I first started out on my own, I ran into many situations outside my comfort zone. I relied on some mental programming techniques using visualization, written goals and powerful word-picture affirmations revolving around opportunity. An affirmation projects your vision into your subconscious through the power of words. *(For additional resources, free tools, special reports and more information on mental programming techniques, visit www.KahunaPower.com)*

I used an inexpensive tape recorder to create a recording of affirmations I developed for myself, along with a few that I borrowed from others. I mixed them together using classical and relaxing music on one side and strong, aggressive music on the other side. Then I listened daily. Most of the affirmations weren't true – yet – but that's the point. Affirmations point the way to where you want to go. My new beliefs birthed actions and soon, many of those affirmations became my new reality.

As a surfer of change, affirmations are a terrific way to help yourself get in the habit of embracing new beliefs about your abilities and goals. Here are some of my favorite affirmations, though by no means are you limited to these. Use them as inspiration to come up with new ones that apply to your unique situation. Try saying them out loud with emotion and you will be amazed at how your mood changes.

Carpe Aqualis! Surfer Affirmations

- I acknowledge NO LIMITS on my abilities and my ultimate success.
- I turn challenges into opportunities.
- I am creative and adaptable to any situation and make the best of whatever comes my way.
- I seek out new opportunities to learn and to grow.
- I always increase my value to other people.
- I see people not how they are, but rather as they can become and work to help them unlock their hidden potential. I am a developer of people.
- I enter into every activity with success in mind. I give no mental recognition to the possibility of defeat.
- I expect challenges and obstacles and am prepared mentally to grow from each challenge before me.
- Every challenge I overcome makes me stronger.
- I am flexible and adaptable in every situation. I look for creative alternatives and seek out new ways of accomplishing my goals.
- Organized activity powered by enthusiasm creates power to succeed in anything I do.
- When problems and difficulties come my way, I do not hide. I boldly attack.

- I am audacious in my relentless pursuit of my goals.
- Opportunities flow to me like the waves of a raging surf.
- I am a *Carpe Aqualis!* surfer, adaptable to any challenge and ready to seize the wave!

The interesting thing is, many of these affirmations are now on autopilot in my life. Some of the things I did not believe I could do, I now can. This allows me to move on to more challenging waves. Does your belief system empower or sabotage you? Do you find yourself thinking or saying things like:

- "That's just how I am."
- "I am just not a morning person."
- "I'm not smart enough."
- "I could never do that."

What phrases and affirmations do you repeat in your mind? Do they build your confidence as a surfer or do they minimize you and lead to a pessimistic viewpoint? Two people might look at the same waves of change and see completely different things. Why is that? It's a good bet that the person who sees opportunity has an inner dialogue that's about ability, competence, and the strength to overcome obstacles. Which voice is whispering in your ear?

Navigate the Hazards and Avoid the Riptide

A riptide is a strong current of water heading back out to sea. It is a significant hazard to swimmers and surfers. You can't out swim a riptide no matter how strong a swimmer you are. To get out, you swim parallel to the shore. Eventually you will swim out of the area of strong currents and can work your way back to shore.

In the same way that people drown trying to swim against a riptide, people swim against their passion or their purpose in life and drown their dreams. When change or opportunity hits you like a riptide, change your course. Forget fighting the change. Swim to the opportunity.

Surf -Titude:

"Who you are is more important than what you do. Focus on who you want to be and what you want to do rather than be disappointed in where you are or what you don't have. Be happy with who you are today, knowing tomorrow you will improve and be even better!"

Chapter *10*

Rule 7 – Go Big or Go Home!
To be Great, You Have to be
Willing to Wipe Out!

Surf -Titude:

"Whatever you can do, or dream you can, begin it! Boldness has genius, power and magic in it. Concerning all acts of initiative and creation, there is one elementary truth - the moment one definitely commits oneself then providence moves too."
– Goethe (1749-1832)

What do Thomas Edison, George Washington Carver, Henry Ford, Alexander Graham Bell and the Wright brothers have in common? They were all failures. All great inventions are really the result of a series of intelligent failures. Each was preceded by countless failures, allowing the inventor to discover what did and did not work. It is estimated that Thomas Edison tried over ten thousand different materials before discovering that a tungsten filament in a vacuum would create light without catching on fire. Failure is part of discovery and discovery is part of learning.

Do you desire a rich, exciting, bold life with thrilling highs and humbling lows? Or would you rather play it safe, avoiding failure at all costs with your only goal to keep plodding forward? To be a great surfer, you must be willing to be a bad surfer. You must be willing to wipe out. Greatness in any endeavor is built on the foundation of failures. Fail forward, learn, analyze, improve and repeat. Shoot for unrealistic expectations. You may fall short, but the preparation you undertake is groundwork for other successes. Why not shoot for a big splash? If you are going to wipe out, at least make it interesting.

Success is Found in Personal Responsibility

Failure is the first stage of success. It is an opportunity to learn and begin again with deeper insight and an improved plan. It is important to realize how significant failure is as part of your success strategy. Nothing you have achieved in your life has come without failure as a precursor. To find more success, fail more often. Of course, you can fail intelligently.

I have made plenty of mistakes in my life and career. Each time I fail, I take personal responsibility for learning from them. Do not be ashamed to make mistakes or admit being wrong. I tell my children the same thing my parents told me growing up. They said no matter what I did or whatever mistakes I made, they would stand by me. But there was one condition: that I was always honest with them. Don't go out of your way to make foolish mistakes, but when you do, own them. Take responsibility, clean it up then move forward.

Perspective Learning Forward™ (Controlled Crashing)

What does surfing have in common with jumping out of airplanes? Both taught me lessons about using failure and setbacks to my benefit. Both have strategies, skills and techniques to essentially deal with failure.

PLF is a military acronym for the *parachute landing fall* technique I learned at the Army Airborne School at Ft. Benning, Georgia, in the summer of 1986. I have since adapted the acronym to *Perspective Learning Forward* or P.L.F. I use it when I fail, crash or wipe out in life. This is a direct application of the **Forward Focus** aspect of the S.U.R.F. Strategy.

Airborne School is three, long, intense and grueling weeks of rigorous physical training, a hot Georgia summer and an instructor in your face most of the time. We had to master how to rig our chutes, how to load and exit the aircraft, how to maneuver our parachutes while in the air, and how to clear the landing zone. But what we spent the most time on was the skill of controlled crashing.

A parachute only slows you down enough so you do not crash into the earth at terminal velocity. However, there is still considerable speed when you land. Maybe you have seen sport parachuting and how fast their approach is. In the last few seconds, they pull down on cords to collapse the chute and slow it down. With the exception of elite units, most of the army parachutes do not have this feature and there is little you can do to slow your descent rate. Even with a parachute, your impact is about the same as jumping from twelve to eighteen feet without a parachute.

Over time, the Army has perfected a method of landing to absorb and distribute the impact of the fall and lessen the effect of the crash. This technique, known as a parachute landing fall, or PLF, allows the body to collapse to distribute the impact over several points of contact, rather than landing only on your feet and doing severe damage to yourself. The PLF is about position upon impact. Each point of contact must come in the right order and with the correct form to allow the body to act as a collapsible spring. The correct position coming in is feet and knees together. The correct order of points of contact are feet, then side of lower leg, then side of quadriceps, then buttocks, and finally back. All this happens quickly in a fluid, collapsing motion.

We spent days practicing this from every imaginable angle. Because you are a passenger of the wind and do not control your direction, you need to prepare to execute a PLF in any direction. Front PLF, left PLF, side PLF – again and again we would practice falling. We slid down cables and did PLFs in the sawdust. They had a sadistic device called a swing-landing trainer that started you on a platform about eight feet high. Wearing a harness attached to a pulley system, you were swung into motion by an instructor. At the instructor's whim, he would let go, forcing you to do a perfect PLF... or do it again and again and again. We drilled and drilled on how to fall, culminating in a drop from a parachute hooked up to a 250-foot tower that pulled you up and then dropped you like an amusement park ride on steroids. This was the last step before jump week and was the pure essence of Terro-Phoria – exhilarating and terrifying. Drills, training and practice every day for almost two weeks took the conscious thinking out of the equation and allowed the reaction to be embedded in my subconscious.

I will never forget learning how to fall. This has helped me significantly in my life when I have found myself hurtling toward the ground out of control. Just as the Army uses a PLF to teach soldiers how to fall, we need to practice Perspective Learning Forward in our lives when we fail or feel like life is crashing in around us.

When you feel like you are wiping out, Perspective Learning Forward enables you to take a different view on your situation. Learn from your errors and look ahead to how you can use that knowledge and experience to create a brighter future. This provides you with an advantage over most people who shut down after being wiped out by a failure. P.L.F. helps you confidently get back on your board with your lessons learned.

Henry David Thoreau observed, "It's not what you look at that matters, it's what you see." When you act with purpose and courage, especially in difficult times, you sow the seeds of future success. When you fail, look for ways to adapt and do better. You might just find strength and ability you didn't know you had.

What to Do When You Get "Maytagged"

All surfers have wipe outs. Surfing bigger waves creates bigger risks. When you get caught under a big wave and rolled over and over like you're in a washing machine, you are getting "maytagged." You feel beaten to a pulp, struggling without oxygen. Panic sets in as you are not really sure where *up* is. Now your only focus is survival. It's not a fun experience, but it happens in surfing and in life.

Learn to not take failure personally. People who are optimistic, positive and hopeful tend to see things that happen as external, the result of circumstances rather than some personal failing. Pessimists tend to interpret results as very personal, the result of their not being good enough. You can see how a pattern of that kind of negative thinking would rapidly become debilitating. You'd freeze like a deer in headlights.

When difficulties happen, learn to see them as temporary, as the result of external factors, not as part of who you are. Remember, your response is all you can control. After a wipe out – especially if you get maytagged – apply the S.U.R.F. Strategy to gain perspective learning forward.

Survey situation
Understand options
Respond based on your plan
Forward focus

Take Risks

Without risk, there would be no achievement. All successful people take chances. Meeting new people is a risk. Learning and growing is a risk. Risk precedes reward. But risk doesn't have to be reckless. The reason most people do not take risks and stay in a comfort zone is that they fear the unknown. They assume that risk has to be reckless and filled with the potential for disaster. It doesn't if you're prepared.

Failure and success are like the Chinese symbol for the yin and yang. It is indistinguishable where failure stops and success begins. No person who creates and sustains success does so without failure. Most successful people have a far greater share of failures in their lives than people who are unsuccessful. Failure is a stepping-stone and many times the precursor to success. Failure with redirected energy seeks out possibilities and creates new opportunities. Failing, accepting responsibility and learning from the failure is the essence of failing forward. We all fall down. But falling, or failing, and then not putting the lessons learned to use is a waste of the learning resource.

Most people think entrepreneurs are risk-junkie thrill seekers, but this is a myth. Certainly, there are some high-profile celebrity entrepreneurs like that, but most are not. I am risk-averse. I don't gamble and have never played the lottery. I evaluate risk very differently than most people. For example, of these three pairs of activities, which do you think is more risky, column A or column B?

A		B
Jumping out of an airplane	or	Driving a car?
Fighting fires	or	Eating a hot dog?
Flying an airplane	or	Crossing the street?

In every case, B is riskier. Surprised? Risk is relative. Risk is a feeling of not having control. Many people are terrified of flying in a commercial jet, even though the best-trained pilots in the world are at the controls. Few people are afraid of driving, yet more drivers per thousand are killed than parachutists per thousand, and in 2004 there were zero U.S. fatalities on commercial airlines. People fear flying because they don't have control. If something does go wrong, all they can do is hold on. Is driving a risk? It depends. Are you driving with a well-trained and experienced driver or a sixteen-year-old with two months under his belt? Risk is relative. Smart, calculated risk is essential for moving forward.

Surf -Titude:

"Many people dream of success. To me, success can only be achieved through repeated failure and introspection. In fact, success represents the one percent of your work which results from the ninety-nine percent that is failure."
– **Soichiro Honda, Founder of Honda Motor Company**

Don't Play it Safe – Go Big or Go Home

Unless you have reached the pinnacle of success or been humbled by failure, it is really hard to have real perspective in your life. While dealing with your emotions, you sometimes don't want to let your highs get too high or your lows get too low.

Almost any great accomplishment you can think of has at some moment in its origin been a failure or a door closed that you can point to as the original seed of success. I can now look back at many of the experiences that I classified as failures, and with the clearer perception of time, I can see how each has benefited me. Failure is a label we attach to an event or a set of circumstances. Events in and of themselves have no intrinsic meaning but rather the meaning we create and attach to it.

Anything Worth Doing is Worth Doing Badly

Skill development happens through practice, trial and error. Whether you are attempting to learn a new language or a new computer program, when you begin, you will fail more than you will succeed. Your skill acquisition will start off ugly. Over time, your skill will grow and your results will improve. Everyone learns this at the beginning of life as children until we are conditioned to forget it.

Each failure pays off in experience while sowing future seeds of opportunities. Every failure brings you closer to your next success. Any sales trainer will confirm that in sales, success and failure are interconnected. The law of probability says that your success rate will rise in direct relation to your failure rate. With a good attitude and a learning mentality, each failure increases your success probability.

Surf boldly and audaciously with optimism. Pessimists feel as though the world controls their fate. Optimists know otherwise. They know they remain in control of their attitude and that this leads to actions and ultimately to their results.

Surf -Titude:

"Make Carpe Aqualis! your battle cry every time you are confronted with difficulties or change."

Chapter *11*

Translating the S.T.A.C.K.™ Strategy into Surfing Success

Surf -Titude:

**"Waves represent change. Change
represents opportunity. Carpe Aqualis!
and seize your opportunity!"**

Surfing is a skill of response and reaction positively adapted to use the force of the waves to your benefit. The S.U.R.F. Strategy is a skill to positively adapt to events and changes in your life. The goal in learning this technique is to combine personal responsibility and creative opportunity to maximize whatever situation you find yourself in.

Surfing and the S.U.R.F. Strategy are response based. Now let's look at creating your ideal future and a direct proactive strategy for getting to the outcome you desire. How do you take control of the direction and situations of your life? Become the architect and builder of your dreams and goals.

In my previous book, *Stack The Logs! Building a Success Framework to Reach Your Dreams* (www.stackthelogs.com), I outlined a simple success strategy and framework for success called the S.T.A.C.K. Strategy™. This is the strategy I used in my life to lose more than fifty pounds, become free of all consumer debt, write my first book and build business ideas into a multi-million dollar company. This is a testament to the power of this strategy.

The S.T.A.C.K. Strategy:
Five Steps to Your Desired Outcome

Set your destination and course.
Take immediate action.
Accept results simply as feedback.
Correct your course based on feedback.
Keep on Stacking the Logs! and making progress
to your goal.

One example of the S.T.A.C.K. Strategy in action came in 2002 when my son Frankie was diagnosed with leukemia and successfully treated at St. Jude Children's Research Hospital. I observed the S.T.A.C.K. Strategy in action at St. Jude as they improved the basic cancer survival rate from less than four percent in 1962 to more than eighty percent forty years later! Their continuing success is a great representation of the how the S.T.A.C.K. Strategy works as Danny Thomas and his group of dedicated, visionary, action-oriented believers did it all.

- Set a destination and a course to defeat childhood cancer;
- They Took immediate action in hiring the best scientists, clinicians, researchers and nurses;
- For over forty years of both heartbreaks and triumphs they Accepted feedback to learn what worked and what did not;
- Based on that feedback, they Corrected course to adapt and improve; and
- They Keep stacking the logs of progress toward Danny's dream that, "No child should die in the dawn of life."

Where S.U.R.F. is a response tool, S.T.A.C.K. is a goal accomplishment tool. The S.T.A.C.K. Strategy is the cornerstone business process for Kahuna Business Group in every initiative we undertake. It's simple but powerful. Here is a quick course in S.T.A.C.K. 101:

S.T.A.C.K. 101

Set Your Destination and Course
- Know your desired destination and motivation.
- Know where you are in relation to your objective.
- Plot a course to get from where you are to where you desire to be.

Take Immediate Action
- Know what actions you need to take to get to your objective.
- Take action.
- Keep taking action.

Accept Results Simply as Feedback
- Know where you are in relation to your goals.
- Allow results to be a neutral feedback mechanism for your progress.
- Maintain your motivation to progress to your destination.

Correct Your Course Based on Feedback
- Change or adapt your approach until you are making the progress you want.
- After you make changes, go back to your feedback mechanism for an update.
- If you are on the right course, add more fuel to the fire and maintain your heading.

Keep on Stacking the Logs!
- Sustain patience, persistence and determination to reach your destination.
- Repeat any previous steps as needed, but maintain action until your goal is achieved.

Surfing Success Through The S.T.A.C.K. Strategy

The S.U.R.F. Strategy (Survey, Understand, Respond and Forward Focus) as a response tool parallels the A and C (Accept Feedback and Correct Course) components of the S.T.A.C.K. Strategy. Look at how neatly S.T.A.C.K. fits into the central S.U.R.F. metaphor of *Carpe Aqualis!*

Set Your Destination and Course
- Know where your board is pointed and make sure it is where you want to go.
- Know your destination and motivation.

Take Immediate Action
- Know what wave to ride and put yourself in a position to ride it.
- Paddle like crazy!

Accept Results Simply as Feedback
- **S**urvey situation (from the S.U.R.F. Strategy)
- **U**nderstand options (from the S.U.R.F. Strategy)

Correct Your Course Based on Feedback
- **R**espond based on Your Plan (from the S.U.R.F. Strategy)
- **F**orward Focus (from the S.U.R.F. Strategy)
- Change or adapt your approach until you are making the progress you want. After you make changes, go back to your feedback mechanism for an update. When you know you are on the right course...

Keep on Surfing Your Waves... Carpe Aqualis!
- Sustain patience, persistence and determination to reach your destination.
- Repeat any previous steps as needed.
- Maintain action until your goal is achieved.

Create Your Own Luck

Know what you want. Don't let your dreams and desires be a secret. If you want to drive your life's progress, you must clearly know what you want. If you don't know, how can anyone else know or help you? If you don't know what you want, how can you complain about where the waves take you? If you want something in life, it is up to you to go after it. It will never just come to you.

Goal setting and achievement are not static events. When you set your course and take action, you will be given feedback to S.U.R.F. As you put these two strategies in place, you will find them in synch with each other. Learn to practice them subconsciously in every situation you find yourself in. Don't be stressed or overwhelmed. Go with it and *Carpe Aqualis!* as you take greater control over your future.

Seize opportunity! Take bold and audacious action to elevate yourself as you surf in the Stewardship Pyramid. Action creates activity, which creates choices. Choices create opportunities and results which create more chances for action in a cycle of success. Bold and audacious action creates a chain reaction that will lead you to your destination. Other people may call it luck, but you will know it was your focused plan and deliberate action that brought about your results. No one can do it for you. Remember, "Your world. Your wave!"

Surf -Titude:

"Seize your opportunities created in change!"

Chapter 12

Organizational Success – "Operation Delta!"

Surf -Titude:

"Great teams are built with great individuals of passion, purpose and commitment to the goal and the team itself."

I f you desire to build a great team, start with you. This chapter and the following four share the secrets of great surfers as the basis of building an outstanding organization, even if the organization is just You, Inc.

You are part of several teams. You may be the leader of a large organization, or you may be the leader of a small group. You might be a key member of a unit at work or on a vital parent team leading your children. Even if you don't fall into any of these categories, please realize this, *you are the leader of your own personal services corporation.* As the president of (your full name), Inc., you are where the buck stops and also where the process begins.

A New Approach

Globalization is linking businesses around the world. Jobs are being outsourced at a frenetic pace. Big, slow corporations are dying and being replaced with more efficient companies. The availability of information combined with the ability to virtually shop around the world has turned nearly every product into a commodity.

While the waves of this situation will pound and destroy some businesses, agile and dynamic "surfer" businesses can harness the power of these same changes to propel them to the top. These organizations embrace the change as an opportunity. They have a powerful curiosity about their customers, their industry and themselves. This applies to you as an individual too. The question is: do you want to be a surfer of the change process or a victim of it?

After nine years of fast growth and sometimes out-of-control business, my partners and I reflected upon the past as we planned the upcoming year. We were excited about what we had achieved, and yet we were uncomfortable with how wide the gap was between where we were and where we knew we could be. Individuals and organizations alike find themselves victims of "drift."

Drift is where you stop to look at where you are in relation to where you came from and realize you have arrived there more by the current you have been swept up in rather than by design. With the speed of our lives and our business, we found ourselves caught up in business drift. We set out to revitalize our business based on the S.U.R.F. Strategy. We realized we needed to remain focused on our corporate goals while improving and streamlining every aspect of our business.

Operation Delta!
(Personal/Professional/Organizational)

We looked at various re-engineering and corporate improvement programs and initiatives like Six Sigma™ used by companies like GE®. Unfortunately, after evaluation, we found them to be impractical and inconsistent with our entrepreneurial DNA. Reflecting on how vital this was to our business, we decided to turn our entrepreneurial creativity inwardly... so we created our own program.

In typical Army jargon, we christened our undertaking, "Operation Delta!" Delta in mathematical terms means change or difference. If a variable in a process changes, the change in the result is called the *delta*. In a math equation, seven minus five leads to a delta of two. Delta represents change by design. It is a transition from where you are now to where you desire to be. The foundation of that program is this.

Developing Your Battle Plan

Every military operation starts with the outcome and works backward. The vision of the end result lets planners apply their creativity in designing and employing big picture strategies. Once the strategies are in place, they determine the tactics and specific action steps necessary to achieve the goals. Broken down, it looks like this:

1. Develop the overall plan and big picture first.
2. Figure out the highest-leverage strategies to get you to your goal in the most direct way.
3. Support your strategy with a tactical plan of action.

Operation Delta!
Phase I – Designing Your Destiny

Great answers flow from great questions. The better the question, the better the result. Keep in mind the process as outlined below should be applied to your life as well as to any organization you have a vested interest in. Take time away from your busy day and think about these seven strategic questions. This looks simple, yet few people take the time to think these questions through. One dynamic in the self-improvement process is knowing exactly what you desire your outcome to be. We sometimes get too caught up in the trivial details of the day and lose sight of the vital big picture.

Seven Strategic Questions of Operation Delta!

1. Who are you at the core?	(What are your values?)
2. Who do you want to become?	(What is your vision?)
3. Why are you here?	(Mission)
4. What is your current situation?	(Situation analysis)
5. Where are you going?	(Direction/goals)
6. How will you get there?	(Strategies/action plans)
7. How will you know when you arrive?	(Evaluation)

This process is circular. These questions are part of the beginning process as well as the end result.

Operation Delta!
Phase II – The Four Commandments

The heart of Operation Delta! is about being self-aware. With awareness, it is easier to apply and affect change. Self-awareness and self-knowledge as both an individual and an organization is the critical first step in the planning process. As you begin to look at this assignment, you will notice two aspects focused inwardly as well as two outwardly focused.

I.   Thou Shalt Know Thyself
     →Internal Focus←
II. Thou Shalt Know Thy Client/Customer/Employee
     →Internal Focus←
III. Thou Shalt Know Thy Industry/Marketplace/Company
     ←External Focus→
IV. Thou Shalt Know Thy Competitors
     ←External Focus→

Operation Delta! Phase III – Action!

With Phases I and II in the works, you can begin to create an action plan. Apply the S.T.A.C.K. Strategy to develop a blueprint of what you want to build. When you are living in the process, use the S.U.R.F. Strategy as a response tool to adapt to whatever comes your way.

Look for the highest-leverage and highest-payoff activities as you move forward with action. Break your plans into one of two categories. They are either *innovation* or *optimization* ideas. These two are the yin and yang of business and personal development. Optimization is working inside to improve effectiveness. Innovation means new ideas that grow and expand your opportunities.

- **Optimization** – Finding hidden efficiencies, expense reduction, better processes, more focus, and so on to receive a higher yield from your existing business.
- **Innovation** – New revenue and profit centers leveraged from existing business and relationships.

Optimization is like a farmer who seeks to increase the yield of the farm. Improvements in tractors, efficiencies in fertilizers and pesticides, better seeds, as well as infrared and satellite technology all contribute to increase output and yield. Optimization is about doing things better, faster, cheaper and differently.

Innovation is like finding adjacent farmland to farm or other markets to sell to. Innovation is turning an expense like waste product removal into a profit center like selling it for fuel. Innovation is about being focused on new opportunities in your marketplace.

After World War II, the Japanese auto industry, under the tutelage of Dr. W. Edwards Deming, created a revolution in the auto industry with his theories and methods of optimization. Studying every measurable component of a factory, Dr. Deming became the preeminent efficiency expert. His optimization techniques are still used to this day.

Optimization alone is not enough, as the Japanese auto makers later found out. They had the best, most efficiently produced cars, but not enough people were buying them. American auto makers adapted, finding innovation with minivans and SUVs. U.S. auto makers regained sales, revenues and market share through this innovation. Ironically, this rebalanced the worldwide auto market, taking away the Japanese dominance gained when the U.S. auto makers had been caught sleeping.

Operation Delta! Phase IV – Keep Surfing

The process of Operation Delta! is not a "one and done" process. It is ongoing and really never ending. Every activity in innovation and optimization generates changes that need to be measured. As you "accept feedback" and "correct course," you will be continuously reinventing yourself.

Seek out and apply new ideas, even the ones that seem crazy. Great ideas sometimes start there. Be strong enough to change and be fluid enough to adapt to opportunities. Business plans can no longer be rigid or static. They must allow room to adapt and change with the challenges as a dynamic planning process. If you are a leader or manager within an organization struggling to tie your big picture into a daily system while managing your team, visit www.KahunaPower.com for resources and information on planning systems designed to create a big picture blueprint while coordinating your activities.

In the next three chapters, we'll take a look at the three qualities it takes to become a great surfer and to build an organization of surfers. Moving ahead, you will discover the top three keys every organization must use to unlock the vault of ongoing success.

1. How to be a great surfer
2. How to attract great surfers
3. How to develop surfing greatness in others

Surf -Titude:

**"Great surfing starts in the mind!
Develop the Carpe Aqualis! mind-set as
you approach every aspect of your life
and work."**

Chapter 13

How to be a Great Surfer –
12 Characteristics of Great Surfers

Surf -Titude:

"A Carpe Aqualis! surfer is opportunity-driven yet centered in personal responsibility. Make a big splash and own it!"

You, Inc., Becoming an Entrepreneurial Surfer!

Whether you earn minimum wage or are in the top bracket of income earners, your business entity, You, Inc., is at the heart of your earning. In a job, you package and market your talents, skills, abilities, attitudes and efforts into something traded to your employer for income. This is no different from being self-employed. The quickest route to earning more money is to recognize your situation and to provide more value to your organization. The more you develop your skills, talents, abilities, attitudes and efforts into value for your employer or your clients, the more you earn and are worth.

Working with other business owners and as an employer myself, I can tell you the most desirable characteristics to find in an employee. Skill and talent are certainly important, but they are only a beginning. The most important characteristics revolve around attitude. Employees who have a positive attitude, are willing to learn and grow, and who take initiative to advance goals or take away headaches are at the top of my list. These employees provide a business with more leverage. They add value. They advance the company's goals and themselves as a result.

If you want to move up, add value to the organization. If you have your own business, do the same for your customers. All of us are hired to serve rather than be served. If you cannot provide value to an organization, why should it continue to employ you? If someone else can provide the same value you do for less money, why should they not replace you with that person?

The key to your potential is to develop and refine the potential of You, Inc. This is not a new concept. It has been used by many people to illustrate how your earning power and production capability rest squarely on *you*. What are you doing to push the boundaries and improve the capabilities of You, Inc.? You don't have to get your education all at once. You do not have to quit your job to go back to school. The key is steady forward motion toward clear goals. Learning is like climbing a mountain. The more you climb, the more you see and the more your perspective improves.

Kahuna A-Player Surfer Characteristics

Put yourself in the role of a leader in your organization with enormous expectations in front of you. The good news is that you will get to select some key players to be part of your team. The bad news is – well, it's the same news. Your responsibility is to identify exactly what you are looking for in these members of your team. Can you envision who you would choose and why? If someone on your team is reading this book, do you think they would rate you as a top pick? What would your company be like if everyone in it were just like you? Teams reflect leadership. How does your team look?

After nearly ten years of growing our business, failure and success in our hiring seemed more luck than science, so our team decided on a different approach. We chose to measure and track success attributes for our existing team, looking for key success traits common with those who excel within our culture. With these common traits of success in our environment more clearly understood and identified, it is now easier for us to uncover the few great surfers to add to our team from the many who might apply.

Listed below is a compilation of surfer attributes and characteristics we determined would assist us in our recruiting. You might not find this list a perfect fit for your situation or company, but it's a great starting point. If your company is a fast-growing, non-traditional organization surfing opportunities in the ever-changing waters of business, you will find this helpful with both individual and organizational perspectives. If you are responsible for hiring or supervising others, you will profit by using and adapting what we have done to develop your own picture of an A-Player surfer.

No matter who provides your paycheck, as "You, Inc.," you will also profit in matching your attributes with those below. By the way, A-Players are never afraid of measuring up against themselves or others. They accept feedback, correct course and keep surfing.

Kahuna A-Player Surfer Characteristics

- **Attitude (positive).** Employees who have a positive attitude seek out ways to succeed instead of internalizing issues and perceived failures.

- **Aptitude (quick learner).** Individuals who have the ability to learn new programs or processes quickly are better prepared to navigate the ever-changing waters of your organization.

- **Scalability (ability to grow and increase responsibilities).** Quick-growth companies often outgrow their staffing needs. Hiring employees

who have the capability and desire to expand
their roles and accept new responsibilities during
transitional periods is a key to growth.

- **Energy (high).** Employees with a high energy
  level are more inclined to attack a challenge
  rather than sit back and react.

- **Communication skills (verbal and non-
  verbal).** This skill is a staple for *any* successful
  business. Clear written, verbal and face-to-face
  communication is crucial in keeping clients
  informed and satisfied and in allowing for
  effective teamwork.

- **Flexibility and adaptability (within current
  positions).** Both are essential in attacking the
  challenging waves that employees encounter
  daily.

- **Subordination of self (willing to bury the ego
  to help the team succeed).** Leadership comes
  from setting an example for others. In our
  environment, leading while being led is not
  uncommon. Our managers and directors support
  their teams while allowing them (and, at times,
  challenging them) to grow.

- **Ambition (hardworking, vision).** Kahuna
  Business Group is unique in that each employee
  is encouraged to be an entrepreneur in his or
  her given roles. Entrepreneurs by nature have
  an internal drive to succeed on their own terms.
  While we do not expect our employees to start
  their own businesses, we do expect them to
  provide the best they have to offer and encourage
  them to question all assumptions.

- **Continuing self-education (always expanding horizons).** While only a handful of Kahuna employees hold degrees from four-year universities, *every* employee takes part in continuing education. Employees who do not believe they have any more to learn are ones that struggle in our fast-paced and ever-changing environment.

- **Leadership.** These people seek solutions when faced with challenges and accept responsibility for self-leadership and for helping others.

- **A "get it done" mentality.** Once they are in the daily flow of our business, employees are expected to make decisions and solve problems. In fact, when bringing an issue to a supervisor for discussion, employees are expected to bring possible solutions as well.

- **Belief in the organization's mission.** If your employees don't "buy into" the message and mission of your organization, they will not take ownership of their position. Without personal ownership, employees will lack the passion and desire to succeed themselves or to help the company succeed.

You Don't Have to Quit Your Job to be an Entrepreneur!

Your position exists to provide leverage and value to your company. It is your responsibility to understand your boss and company as clients and then to exceed their expectations. Your value is based on your experience, knowledge, skill-set, aptitude and your effort in coordinating all of your resources.

Do not wait for things to happen. Set yourself apart from the crowd and make things happen. Take initiative and take a chance. Your strategy should be to determine which areas deliver maximum benefit for the investment of your time, effort and energy. Do not spend time and effort dwelling on your limitations or what you cannot do. Instead, look to magnify and capitalize on your strengths and potential.

Leverage and separating yourself from the pack comes from consistently doing things that offer you the highest leverage and highest payoff. Most people look outwardly for success. They look for someone else to appreciate them, someone else to promote them, someone else to motivate them. *Success is not external shining in; it is internal radiating out.* If you want a promotion, set up the conditions to get promoted.

The Secret of Upward Corporate Mobility (Getting Promoted)

You were hired to get specific results. Your paycheck is a trade off for a specific amount and quality of work. As your work is put together with others on your team, value is created in the marketplace.

Most people don't understand the value they are trading for their paycheck. But when you are clear about why you are on the organizational chart and the results you were hired to produce, it is much easier to perform at your peak. As you add more value, you can expect to get paid more and promoted sooner.

Do you know the essential characteristics and skills you must possess to continue to add value to your organization? Can you pinpoint the key factors that will determine how far you can go in your job? Do you know the measuring stick to determine success or failure in your job? If you do, you can transform your skill-set to bury the needle on the company meter and make yourself invaluable.

Reinvest in Your Success

As you learn to live a Carpe Aqualis! life, you'll earn more money. What you do with that money is critical. You could spend it on consumption or use it as negative leverage to get deeper into debt. Or you could create a success habit of reinvesting some of it in your greatest wealth building asset...YOU! This might mean education, equipment, learning resources or any number of other tools. Investment back into you will in turn make you even more valuable and further increase your earning power. It is a wonderful success cycle that pays significant compound interest.

It amazes me how many people will pay tens of thousands of dollars for a college education and then not spend any money on continuing education or skills training. This makes no sense. Sadly, most people stop learning after their formal education.

Education helps you provide more value than others expect. As you do this in every relationship and business transaction, you build your foundation for success based on the sowing and reaping, service, and in creating abundance. Your reward comes from your service to others. Give more than you are asked to give and you will receive more than you expected.

Waves in Motion

You are a surfer and an individual entrepreneur completely responsible for You, Inc. Your security is not in your company or in your industry or in your education, family, alma mater or in anything external. Your security is in yourself as a surfer able to adapt and utilize your skills, talents and abilities with whatever wave of opportunity or change is breaking before you.

Understand that the base of our lives, our situation, and our future results are our personal responsibility. Your success will be in proportion to your personal responsibility. No one will do it for you. Luck and serendipity do not just happen; they follow the law of cause and effect. Personal responsibility is at the heart of manufacturing your own luck. The harder you work and the more personal responsibility you take for every situation in your life, the more the law of sowing and reaping and the law of cause and effect will work to your benefit. As this wave begins to swell on the ocean and rise in a slow crescendo toward you, it is *your* opportunity to *Carpe Aqualis!*

Surf -Titude:

"Success is not external shining in; it is internal radiating out."

Chapter 14
How to Attract Great Surfers

Surf-Titude:

*"Luck definitely plays a part in success.
Luck is created in bold, determined
action in the direction of your objective.
Don't wait for your wave. Seize it!"*

Finding, Engaging and Keeping Great People is the Heart of Organizational Success

Any success that I enjoy today I can trace back to two specific lessons I learned the hard way. The first was that to find riches, you must enrich others. The second, organizational success is also achieved in helping others succeed. This truly is the "rising tide lifts all surfboards" concept. Why are most managers intimidated by the success of their subordinates, as if they were going to be overshadowed? How shortsighted this view is.

One of my greatest strengths is my complete average-ness. I do not have any one strength so outstanding I can completely rely on it. Instead, I do my best where I am strong and I rely on my teammates where I am not. I love being on a team. *A great team will magnify its member's strengths and compensate for their weaknesses.*

A great team doesn't need a single superstar carrying the rest of the team. Great teams are balanced and focused. Think about the quote, "We achieve our victories through the victories of those we serve." If you are a leader, your victories will only come as a result of the victories of your team.

Team Surf -Titude:

"Great teams magnify, build on and multiply each other's strengths and talents while working around, managing and minimizing individual weaknesses."

Become an Entrepreneurial Surfer Organization

There is a sarcastic observation about business: business would be great if it were not for two things – customers and employees. Some businesses really do act like customers and employees are a "necessary evil" with the only goal of making money. Profit is certainly a major goal of business, but it can't be the only goal.

Some employees work just hard enough to not get fired, playing it safe while buying into the notion of entitlement and what is owed to them. Of course this is in direct conflict with the organization that pays their people just enough so they will not quit, offering them nothing more than a commodity to take or leave until something better comes along.

The pendulum of corporate control was far to one side after World War II until the birth of the information age which was benchmarked by the fall of the Berlin Wall. The norm was to work for one company right out of school until retirement. The gold watch and the company pension gave way to a pendulum swing far in the other direction where loyalty to a single company is almost non-existent. The old norm was extremely linear, moving from education to career and progressing only within a narrow focus. Now the new norm is education to job, re-education to different job, creating a career path that zigzags sometimes not just in and out of companies but also in and out of different industries.

Entrepreneurial surfer companies who balance their corporate needs and the needs of those who are on their team develop success through the success of the balanced team. It does not matter whether you are a solo worker, consultant, non-profit, club, organization, small business or large company. The secret of organizational success is to create a surfer's environment of *intrepreneurship*. This allows people to play to their strengths and passions to contribute inside the organization, affecting change no matter where they sit on the organizational chart.

The leader's job is to find and attract talented people and integrate them into your culture, mission, vision and values. Notice I said *integrate* not *assimilate*. Organizations who seek to assimilate, rob themselves of the unique education, experiences, background and approach of people they bring to their team.

Avoid inbreeding. Don't allow your team to be a group of clones all agreeing with each other or with you. Seek those who will challenge and innovate while staying on the same course as the rest of the team. This is *alignment*. Keep in mind, alignment is not agreement, with a bunch of fake-smiling, nodding-head, yes people. Our team has many spirited discussions and passionate debates. Our leadership team has both permission and an obligation to provide candid feedback. We also have an agreement to subordinate our egos in the interest of team alignment, even if we do not always personally agree with the direction. Functional and growing teams will have discord and will not always agree. That's natural and healthy. As long as you're aligned toward the same goals, some constructive disagreement keeps things fresh, vital, innovative and challenging.

The Difference between Leadership and Management

Managers direct activity. They get the team moving and coordinate activities to achieve results. Managers are important. Someone has to get people working, direct their efforts and ensure they and the mission stay on track. But that's not leadership.

Leaders take obstacles away, provide guidance and direction from their vision, and set the emotional thermostat. Leaders help people be the best they can be. A true leader will see more in the individuals on a team than the individuals may see in themselves. Good managers manage; great managers lead.

Always lead first, manage second. Even if you don't have anyone reporting to you, provide an example through leadership of yourself on a daily basis. Leadership at every level must be earned. It can't be conferred by a title or position. A company's CEO might be its top manager, but a lower-level department head might be the one everybody turns to for leadership that inspires and elevates. There is a difference.

People take their cues from leaders. This is what leadership expert John Maxwell cites as the "Law of the Lid." The efforts, standards and results of the team will almost never exceed those of its leader. So it's on you to set your standards high – results, efficiency, punctuality, your personal dress code and adoption of an attitude of service and performance in everything you do.

If you're not a formal leader now, act like one and be a leader of yourself. If you want to attract other great surfers, be a great surfer first. Like attracts like. We magnetize the conditions we seek. The best and most satisfying victories come through serving other people. Set the example. Other surfers who share your passion and commitment will be drawn to you.

Surf -Titude:

"Like attracts like. To attract great surfers... be one."

Chapter *15*

How to Develop Surfing Greatness in Others

Surf -Titude:

"Your life will not develop by what life gives you; it will be created by what you do with what life gives you. Destiny is not found in the raw materials life provides us; it is forged in our creation and what is built out of the opportunities we are presented with."

Every day you are greeted by opportunity. Knowing your response to opportunity is the beginning of surfing greatness. Learn to be fluent in the language of opportunity. As you become proficient in this new language and learn to see opportunities in every situation, your career path will definitely be affected. The most satisfying thing about learning a new language is to practice and share with others. Sure, it may be a little clumsy at first, but remember, anything worth doing well is worth doing poorly... at first.

The best way to learn is through teaching and mentoring others. You do not have to wait to be anointed with some expert status or reach a certain level on the organizational chart to teach and mentor others. As you begin preparing ideas to share with others, your mind will move to a new level. As you communicate with and teach others, the concepts you share begin to crystallize into mastery. The knowledge in your mind should never be static. You are either growing or you are dying. There is no better way to maintain growth than to teach and build others with your newfound knowledge and skills.

Your Role as Surfing Instructor

Share what you know to make your team stronger. Don't be stingy with your knowledge and your experience. Don't feel threatened by the success of those you teach. Instead, let this be a validation of you as a teacher and mentor for others. There is no better way to employ what you have learned than to immediately apply it, and there is no better way to apply concepts than to share them with others. As discussed earlier, adding value and building up others will not hold you back. Teaching and building others demonstrates your ability to lead.

As I mentioned in Chapter 1, I am learning Spanish, but just reading a book about Spanish *es no bueno*. Learning comes from applying and using your new words and concepts. Speaking and conversing allows you to begin to make a language of your own. As I learn new words, I share my discoveries with my children and I take my new knowledge to a higher level. Teaching and sharing a new concept forces me to learn differently. Ultimately, it makes my learning experience more practical and applicable.

Discover the Strengths of Others and Assist Them to Surf to Those Strengths

To develop surfing greatness in others, it is vital to help them first see it in themselves. Most people are loaded with self-doubt and a hundred reasons why they don't deserve, don't qualify or don't believe in themselves. German philosopher and author Wolfgang von Goethe observed, "Treat a man as he is and he will remain as he is. Treat a man as he can and should be, and he will become as he can and should be."

Truer words were never spoken when it comes to mentoring others. Expect greatness from others. Learn to see people as they can be. Nurture greatness in others even (especially) when they do not see it in themselves. Leaders take away the oxygen that fuels the fires of doubt and insecurity.

Regardless of who you work for or who works for you, you must communicate to people your belief in them. When you clearly communicate your vision of what your team – and the individuals on your team – can become, you will move mountains. Think of Mel Gibson as William Wallace in the movie *Braveheart* – a brave and charismatic leader among his people. His victories came from vividly sharing his vision of freedom and the value of what they were fighting and dying for. He built an army by sharing a vision of what they could do and the triumphs they were destined to accomplish.

If you have never had a leader inspire you to your greatest potential, become that leader yourself. Inspire others. If you have never had anyone believe in you or mentor you, this is your great opportunity. Not only will you be able to provide this for yourself, you will give a wonderful gift to those who work for and with you. Managers who are feared produce low morale and turnover. Leaders who inspire produce enthusiasm and passion.

Organizations need leadership and vision from the top down, but they need input, feedback and support from everywhere inside. No matter where you are in the company strata, you can make an impact.

What You Do is Not Nearly as Important as Who You Are!

Like most companies, we have our mission, vision and values as posters in our office. The mission of Kahuna Business Group is: *Business Development through Leverage, Value and Partnership. We achieve our victories through the victories of those we serve.* Our vision is: *Enterprise Focused. Opportunity Driven. Carpe Aqualis!* Our mission and vision have changed and adapted as our business has evolved over the last decade. Our values, however, have remained constant.

Guided by our values, we are an evolving and adapting business development company successfully surfing the changing waves of business opportunities within our chosen niche.

- We make choices and decisions every day guided by integrity, ingenuity, common sense and the Kahuna Mission.
- We are accountable for our actions and take personal responsibility for our results.
- We are not afraid to make honest mistakes. We learn from them, move forward and improve as a result.
- We are relentless in the pursuit of our goals. We plan for our success, openly share details with our team, and execute daily.
- We believe in ourselves and each other. We are stronger as a team than as individuals.
- We strive for personal development, professional development and balance in our lives.
- We are loyal to everyone on our team including clients, vendors, partners and each other.
- We view problems and challenges not as obstacles but as opportunities for our success.
- We have fun within all our relationships and enjoy our business while striving towards our goals each and every day.
- We are excited about our business opportunities, knowing that... *the best way to predict the future is to create it!*

Kahuna Business Group originated as an entrepreneurial experiment and is ongoing today. My partners and I have all had other jobs, working for other companies and observing every element of corporate good, bad and ugly. We knew we would never create utopia or some perfect society, but we realized something vital early on: *What we do is not nearly as important as who we are!* We set out to develop a business based upon a common set of values and a realization that we were not bound by traditional concepts. With a business name like Kahuna located in central Illinois, you are almost *expected* to be a little non-traditional.

Our business has adapted to several industries and continues to S.U.R.F. new opportunities. Our biggest realization is in our core values and our entrepreneurial DNA. We know who we are. This gives us confidence that even if something happens to the economy or our main industry, our team would be able to adapt and survive. We are confident in our belief that who we are trumps what we do. We realize and embrace the belief that within our ongoing business experiment we can design and build our ideal long-term company. As surfers, we understand we are all alone yet bound together by the values and ambitions we share.

Share and Communicate Your Vision and Expectations of a Bright Future

For many companies, the display of mission, vision and values is more artwork for the company walls or the annual report than a genuine sharing of vision and purpose. Having a great slogan does not make a great company. Great companies are born from passion, energy, shared goals, and a sense that everyone contributes and has the potential to rise as far as his or her ability and drive will take them. That's a lot more than a poster slogan.

To say our Kahuna team is unique would be a bit of an understatement. Earlier this year, Kelly and Brianne, two motivated teammates from completely different areas of our business, came up with a unique idea. Rather than just an ordinary poster to blend into the scenery like corporate wallpaper, they asked, "Why not do something really bold and way out of our comfort zone to share who we are and what we believe?" Their idea was to design and create a large quilt to display our mission, vision and values.

What began as an offhand comment, starting with the words, "Wouldn't it be cool if..." created a spark of initiative and hard work for a massive three-section quilt covering over 117 square feet. Over nine feet in length, the Kahuna Quilt has taken on a life of its own. It incorporates our corporate image and communicates who we are, where we are going and what we believe. The quilt demonstrates where we have come from and the path we are heading down.

A quilt is a perfect metaphor for a company's culture. It is made up of many individual team members, each with his or her own color, pattern and texture. Each brings different strengths, weaknesses, passions, talents, backgrounds, points of view and attitude to the organization. Together, they combine to make a unique tapestry.

For us the Kahuna Quilt represents a simple truth: who we are is more important than what we do. Who we are collectively is much more than the sum of our individual parts. Not everyone could survive in our slightly-zany, fast-paced, self-directed, and sometimes out-of-control, Terro-Phoria, crazy environment. We know who we are and who we are not. Any new person who considers joining our team will have no doubt where we stand. The environment our team thrives on would be the wrong ecosystem for someone looking for status-quo, traditional, corporate, business as usual, predictable and clearly defined. Likewise, most of us would be surfers out of water in a different corporate environment. Our culture is not necessarily better; it is just better for us.

The symbolism of regular individuals as fabric coming together to enhance and enrich and create a work of art has meaning as each of us can see the contribution we make to the end result. To see our Kahuna Quilt, or for more information, please visit www.KahunaPower.com/quilt.

As a leader, develop a clear vision of what you represent and where you are going. Others will follow you, and as they begin to see a vision of what they can become, you will be able to train them to surf. Create a compelling vision of the future and you will be surprised who will follow.

Celebrate Great Rides

You have been preparing for months. You are in position and you are ready. A swell develops and begins to transform before your very eyes. A monster wave is now bearing down upon you. Your training and instincts kick in as you paddle as if you were racing it. You apply all of your skill and training as you find yourself standing and then suddenly dropping down a mountain of angry water. You maintain your balance and you handle your wave with great skill and superb style. You avoid the hazards, even though you have a few moments when you are not sure you are going to make it. But you do make it. You ride through to where the wave finally breaks on the shore. Awesome!

When you have a great ride, celebrate it! It's an event to be commemorated. Reflect and share the joy with your team. Rejoice in the great rides and build on each other's successes. Learn from each other and discuss what you can learn from your victories. Use the adrenaline boost from your great rides to give you momentum and victories to build on. Remember them for confidence when the surfing is difficult.

Use Mistakes and Setbacks to Build and Strengthen Your Team

Okay, so maybe instead of riding that monster wave to shore, you lose your nerve and end up battered in the washing machine, surfacing covered in scrapes and bruises, and wondering what the heck just happened. Get used to it. It happens to the best of surfers.

Every person or team with ambition will experience failure. Just as every wipe out teaches you lessons as an individual, disappointments can also provide your team with experience and perspective.

Make no mistake, you *will* wipe out. The only way to avoid it is never to challenge the surf and never to leave your comfort zone. That's far worse than failure. Apply the S.T.A.C.K. Strategy to accept feedback and correct course any and every time your team has a setback or wipe out. Do an after-action report and work with your team to learn from the experience and apply the lessons learned to the future.

Surf -Titude:

"Failure without learning is still failure. Failure with learning is experience!"

Demonstrate and Expect Loyalty

A team of great surfers cannot exist without trust and loyalty. We have hundreds of opportunities to demonstrate loyalty to those we serve above, below and beside us on the organizational chart. From being courteous to just holding your tongue when you have the urge to gossip, trust and loyalty grow one interaction at a time. They are eroded and destroyed the same way.

In big wave surfing, trust and loyalty come in the form of those jet ski riders who tow surfers out of the way of killer waves. A surfer must trust the rider to bail him out when things go bad. In your business life, it may not be life and death, but no person can achieve anything without the help of others.

The bank account of trust and loyalty always shrinks or grows. Every transaction you have from those around you either grows your wealth of trust and loyalty or makes a withdrawal. Loyalty is easy when things are good. But when difficulties come, if your balance is zero, who will still be standing beside you?

Loyalty is a choice. Loyalty is being honest even when it is uncomfortable. Loyalty is pushing people out of their comfort zone with a vision of the greatness they may not see in themselves. Loyalty is appreciating others. It is adding value to others. Loyalty comes from your everyday actions and interactions. You don't have to speak a single word to be communicating. Actions don't speak, they scream!

All Alone... Together!

Before you can lead or motivate others, you must learn to lead and motivate yourself. Every surfer is an individual. You are alone, and yet you are part of one or more teams. In truth, we are all alone... together. Developing surfing greatness in others is about the leadership of self.

Every interaction with someone either brings them up or takes them down. Learn to make every opportunity count and find ways to always build others. This is the essence of attracting, developing and keeping great surfers. Achieve your victories by adding value to others, and you will see the tide lift all surfboards. Surfing is individual, but it is certainly more fun and fulfilling when you can share it with others!

Surf -Titude:

"Be a catalyst to enable the success of others and you will find your success naturally."

Chapter 16

What Color is Your Surfboard?

Surf -Titude:

"True success in any endeavor is found in the powerful combination of opportunity awareness grounded in the realization of ultimate personal responsibility. Carpe Aqualis! Your World. Your Wave!"

In our ongoing surfing theme, the waves represent change and opportunity. The board is the metaphor for the vehicle to bring the surfer to the surf. Your board is the connection between your surfing skills, talents, abilities and attitudes and the waves of change and opportunity. Your board is your leverage in the surfing process. A surfboard alone is meaningless, just as a great surfer could not effectively surf on a sheet of plywood. Both elements are important, but it is the combination that is vital.

Prepare Yourself to be a Great Surfer

What do you get when you mix great waves of opportunity with a disciplined surfer on a first-class board of skills, talents and abilities who is waxed with a great and positive attitude? You get great surfing. Your life as a surfer is shaped by persistent waves of change and opportunity. Being a

Carpe Aqualis! surfer is about learning and using the skills to maximize the waves. Why is it that the same wave can wipe out some surfers and yet give others a tremendous ride? The answer is not in the waves. The answer is in the surfer.

Life is challenging. You will constantly find yourself in a state of change. Every day will challenge you more than the day before. There is more for you to keep up with, learn and adapt to. As change affects your life, you can ignore, resist, follow or surf it as a leader. If you ignore or resist, the change will still come, and you'll either be blind-sided or battered by the surf.

Be both a follower and a leader at the same time. This may seem like a contradiction, but it is not. Follow the rules of society, follow your supervisor, follow your clients and customers, follow your goals. Then lead with initiative and an awareness of opportunity grounded in personal responsibility. Understand your mission and your rules of engagement, then take action to accomplish your mission. Apply creativity and initiative at every opportunity. Learn and adapt when you don't get the immediate results you want. Be tenacious and be consistent.

Clint Eastwood delivered a great line in his 1986 movie, *Heartbreak Ridge*, demonstrating the tenacity of the Marines. As gruff, battle-tested Gunnery Sergeant Highway, he is put in a position to train new troops who may go into battle. In the most memorable line of the movie, he offered wisdom in which they could trust their lives: "Improvise, adapt and overcome!" This was his philosophy; accomplish your mission even when your plan falls apart because of the chaos on the battlefield. The military is always adapting. Great companies are always adapting. Smart people in every endeavor are always adapting. Why? Because things rarely go as planned. Over, under, around or even through, you've got to think on your feet, be tough, and never, ever quit.

Choose to lead and to be a leader regardless of your position or job title. Learn how to respond positively to change and the unknown. It does not matter if your business card says CEO, president, director, manager, supervisor, or if you don't even have one. If you are an investor, business owner, minister, administrative assistant, salesperson, soldier, self-employed, stay-at-home parent, nurse, inventor, small business owner or student, this applies to you. Do not allow yourself to be trapped in fear of the waves. Master them!

A Tale of Two Franks

Action, initiative and an opportunity orientation combined with personal responsibility provides a winning formula for success. Opportunity and responsibility are the two vital traits for an entrepreneurial *Carpe Aqualis!* surfer. This is clearly illustrated in the difference between my late father (Frank III) and myself (Frank IV).

The Pitfalls of Plodding Personal Responsibility

My father was a disciplined, hard worker. He was a combination of scientist and salesperson. He consulted and sold chemicals along with water treatment solutions for large companies and municipalities. My dad was a gifted, six-foot-four-inch athlete, and he was always the center of attention with his larger-than-life personality. After a couple of years in the Army gave him a lesson in maturity, he finished college, majoring in both business and science. He was tremendously disciplined and focused in everything he ever did. Although he was a skilled salesperson with a high IQ, his OQ (opportunity quotient) was low. He was old school and very proud of his straightforward approach of: "Keep stacking the logs!" His PRQ (personal responsibility quotient) was at the high end of the scale... practically off the scale.

He attempted one venture into opportunity by partnering with some friends to open a motorcycle shop in the mid 1970s. Unfortunately, the economy went bad, oil prices rose and interest rates soared. The interest on the money to buy and display motorcycles was more than what they were bringing in. They were forced to sell out to a competitor. He never took such a risk again. He reverted to his trusted attitudes. Stick with what you know. One log at a time. Risk is gambling. Find a good company and put in your thirty years.

My father passed away in 1998, and I know he was content and happy in the love of his family. I do believe, however, that because of this event, he left some of his ambition and passion in a box that was never opened.

The Perils of Undisciplined Opportunity

As a young man, I was a dreamer. I was an explorer and left on my own quite a bit. I wanted to be like my dad and I wanted my dad's attention. I discovered a natural inclination and talent for sales, usually winning every sales contest I entered. I listened to dad's motivational and inspirational sales tapes, and I read books about success. I did okay in school and in sports, but I never really excelled at either. I went away to college and immediately took that freedom as a challenge to develop new moneymaking opportunities. I came up with ideas for campus businesses and new ways of making money. I was all over the place and always changing my focus. I thought I was a young entrepreneur. In reality, I was an opportunity seeker without real discipline. My *Carpe Aqualis!* profile was unbalanced with a very high *opportunity quotient*, but a low personal *responsibility quotient*. Like many young people, I lacked seasoning and life experience.

I dropped out of college in the middle of my junior year, certain I would be a multi-millionaire as soon as one of my ideas took off. I had ambition and possessed tremendous opportunity awareness. I had short bursts of success. I went into every situation certain it would end up great with riches and rewards to spare. As a trained salesperson with energy and enthusiasm, I was never fired, but I could not hold a job for more than a few years. I jumped from opportunity to opportunity, always certain this current one was *the one*.

What kept me from success in my early years was not a lack of skills, talents, abilities or attitude. My *personal responsibility quotient* was underdeveloped and unable to support my opportunity ambitions. I lacked a foundation of focus, discipline, follow-through, self-awareness – traits I have only developed today through some hard lessons.

It pains me to reflect on that part of my life. Though I never caused harm on purpose, my wipe outs didn't only affect me. I also sometimes hurt people who followed and believed in me. Without an Opportunity Quotient (OQ) balanced with a strong Personal Responsibility Quotient (PRQ), success will remain elusive.

Determining Your Carpe Aqualis! Orientation

Success in surfing is about balance. Where do you fall on the scales below? The key to applying the S.U.R.F. Strategy is to survey where you are and understand your options and opportunities to then respond with an eye on your goals.

- **High Opportunity Quotient** characteristics include descriptive words like ambition, creativity, adaptability, flexibility, optimism, initiative, dreamer, imagination, ingenuity, visionary and confidence.

- **High Personal Responsibility Quotient** characteristics include descriptions like focus, self-discipline, discernment, wisdom, determination, drive, willpower, resolve, fortitude, judgment and tenacity.

Rate yourself in both categories on a scale of 1 to 10 with 1 being very low, underdeveloped or simply absent. A 10 would indicate you are the poster child for the characteristic.

OQ-Opportunity Quotient:

1   2   3   4   5   6   7   8   9   10

PRQ-Personal Responsibility Quotient:

1   2   3   4   5   6   7   8   9   10

Now plot your numbers on the graph below to see where you are. If you're not happy with your result, don't despair. You can consciously improve your *Carpe Aqualis!* Quotient.

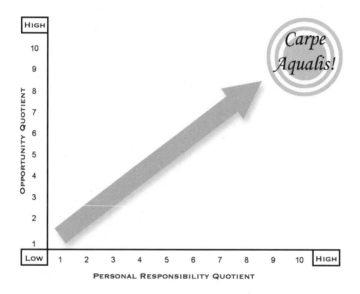

Let's take this one step further and look at the four quadrants of *Carpe Aqualis!* When you look honestly at your profile, you will find yourself in one of four quadrants:

Quadrant 1 (Yellow):
    High Opportunity/Low Personal Responsibility
    (Surf Dreamer/Wannabe)
Quadrant 2 (Green):
    High Opportunity/High Personal Responsibility
    (Carpe Aqualis! Surfer)

Quadrant 3 (Red):
> Low Opportunity/Low Personal Responsibility
> *(Beach Bum/Surf Slacker)*

Quadrant 4 (Blue):
> Low Opportunity/High Personal Responsibility
> *(Shore Line Surfer/Spectator)*

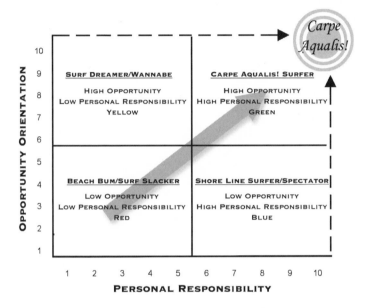

The Pathway to Becoming a Quadrant 2 (Green) Carpe Aqualis! Surfer

There is good news. No matter where you are, there is a path to the upper east side of the chart. Survey where you are. Understand your options and what it will take. Respond based on what you need to work on and how you want to develop. Focus forward to your desired goals, what you want to achieve and a plan to get it done.

Quadrant 1 (Yellow) – High OQ/Low PRQ

These people want the end result but not the work that comes with it. They rely on the lottery or jump around to every grass-is-greener-money-making opportunity. This was me as a young adult. The key to success for people who find themselves in this quadrant is to shore up the personal responsibility area to support their dreams. These are the dreamers, gamblers and opportunists.

One of my partners is a black belt and former karate instructor. He told me how some students would come in wanting to be Bruce Lee, to break bricks or be able to take on a group of thugs. But the mundane, day in and day out practice was too much of a price to pay. The world is filled with this group of people who want to be rock stars, famous athletes, movie stars, wealthy or any of the countless other highest level aspirations without making the commitment and dedication to do whatever it takes to get it done.

To move into quadrant 2, you must work on developing personal responsibility habits big enough to support your ambitions. The bigger your ambitions, the more solid the personal responsibility support structure needs to be for your foundation.

Quadrant 4 (Blue) – Low OQ/ High PRQ

This category is the majority of the workforce. Quadrant 4 people like my father are diligent and hard working, but they do not speak the language of opportunity or recognize it all around them. They play it safe. They are afraid to risk. They wait to be told what to do, then they do it very well. Q4s are reliable, dependable people who you want around you. They are straight-line thinkers and one-foot-in-front-of-the-other workers. But they're missing that "intrepreneurial" drive and initiative to add value.

If you are in this quadrant, you have the foundation of personal responsibility to support your ambition. To move up into quadrant 2, learn to see yourself as an internal entrepreneur and a business within a business. You must develop as a leader, applying new levels of resourcefulness and ingenuity to your role. Learn to appreciate risk and the opportunity for rewards. Push your boundaries and leap out of your comfort zone.

Quadrant 3 (Red) – Low OQ/Low PRQ

People in this quadrant exist based either on the charity of others or on their personality and charm... for now. If you find yourself in this category, time for a life wake-up call. Without opportunity initiative or personal responsibility, you are a freeloader. What organization would possibly want to employ you? Did you even buy this book or did someone get it for you, suggesting you read it?

But there is hope. Many successful people have been here and moved into another quadrant. Perhaps you have never fully had to rely on yourself, or maybe you have always had people to take care of your problems. The path to quadrant 2 begins with changing your attitude and your mind-set about both opportunity and the personal responsibily to support your dreams and ambitions.

What Color is Your Surfboard?

Life will present waves of challenges and opportunities with the power to wipe you out or take you on a tremendous ride. What matters is your approach. People can observe the same wave and come to different yet accurate conclusions. Some will see the waves as problems. Others will see the same wave as opportunity. Same wave, different perception. How do you see the waves of change and your ability to surf?

No matter what your skill level or surfing aptitude is right now, you can learn and apply some simple skills and tools to surf like a pro. In life, there are those who are optimistic. There are also those who are pessimistic. There is really only one difference. An optimist thinks brightly on the future while a pessimist thinks the future will be negative. The reality is this... it is not the event, it is your response to the event that will determine your outcome. The filter of how you interpret what happens to you followed by your response and actions over time will ultimately determine your future.

Remember, knowledge is not power, but *applied* knowledge can be. Success is available for you if you apply the building blocks. Each moment and each day are building blocks upon which you will build your life. If your actions are random, without thought or planning, your ultimate structure will be flawed. It will lack utility and purpose.

When you plan each activity and each goal, like a carefully laid brick upon a solid foundation, the resulting structure will be strong and beautiful. Building blocks for success are habits of success. Small achievements create larger achievements. Small decisions shape the day. Actions of the day compounded over weeks and months and years produce results. The question is, will you allow yourself to remain the laborer in someone else's castle or will you become the architect of your own future?

Building Your Board: Skills, Talents, Abilities, Attitude and Personal Responsibility!

You were born with the abilities that provide you with the power to change your life. You possess the ability to learn, adapt and grow beyond what you were born with. You can develop your skills, talents and your attitude. You can and must evolve. A common motivational theme is: "Attitude drives aptitude." I agree, but let's take it to the next level.

Surf -Titude:

"Your Carpe Aqualis! opportunity-based attitude, combined with the "Your World. Your Wave!" personal responsibility will drive your aptitude and determine the results in your life!"

People who are optimistic and hopeful take a different set of actions than people who are negative. Pessimists attract negative results and negative people. They are their own self-fulfilling prophecy. Optimists attract people who energize and empower them, leading to better results that attract more good people.

My business partners and I travel frequently. I cannot remember a trip where we did not find opportunities or sit next to someone on a plane who met a crucial need we had at just that time. We go into every trip and every meeting with the expectation that we will attract exactly what we need... and we usually do. It's amazing! This is not to say that we do not have setbacks, difficulties and even some spectacular wipe outs. Of course we do. We're human. But compared to the opportunities we're able to perceive and create all around us, a few setbacks are nothing.

My mom had a plaque in our kitchen that read, "Even my failures are edible." Every wave gives us something we can use. Every wave can be ridden and cherished. Every change carries with it some kind of gift or lesson... when you train yourself to see it and act upon it. That's the essence of *Carpe Aqualis!*

 # *Parting Surf-Titudes for Your Surf-cess...*

- Waves will come – choose to surf them.
- New waves equal new beginnings.
- Get in the water...you can't surf from the shore.
- It is your wave. Get off your butt, get into position and make it happen!
- Successful surfing starts with personal responsibility.
- Point your board where you want to go – work toward goals, values and ideals.
- Even with a perfect wave, you still have to paddle.
- Adapt and positively respond to whatever the wave gives you.
- A rising tide lifts all boards.
- Be an individual, but remember you are part of a family and community.

- Proficient surfers are prepared – board, wetsuit, sunscreen and knowledge of the area. (breaks, rip tides, coral reefs, rocks, sharks, and other surfing predators).
- Don't quit your wave too soon; but don't ride a bad wave all the way.
- Take risks, find your passion and purpose.
- Master the fine art of the wipe out and fail forward!
- When bad surf happens to good people, weather your storms and look for your blessings in adversity.
- "Your World. Your Wave!" Go big... or go home.
- Surfing is fun... enjoy the ride!

Surf -Titude:

"It is your world. It is your wave. Design it, build it, surf it, enjoy it, live it... CARPE AQUALIS!"

Afterword

Thank you for sharing this journey with us. We hope you will be able to immediately apply these principles to your life and take better advantage of the opportunities that surround you.

"Your World. Your Wave!"
Carpe Aqualis!

For additional resources or to communicate with me directly, please visit our website:

www.KahunaPower.com

Blessings to you!

Sincerely,

Frank F. Lunn IV
Kahuna Empowerment, Incorporated
www.KahunaPower.com
www.CarpeAqualis.com
Bloomington, Illinois

About the Author

Frank F. Lunn is the President and CEO of Kahuna Business Group, Incorporated, a family of entrepreneurial companies focused on business development grounded in leverage, value and partnership for the clients they serve.

With annual revenues over twenty-five million dollars per year, Lunn is a respected authority on leadership, motivation and opportunity, who understands how to make change a constructive force in life. An expert leader, marketer, small business entrepreneur and author of *Stack The Logs! Building a Success Framework to Reach Your Dreams*, Lunn brings great perspective to teaching others his proven methods for success.

–Photographs by Karla Jenkins Studio

Lunn attended Illinois State University majoring in economics with a minor in military science. Commissioned in 1987 as an officer in the U.S. Army, he served in the Persian Gulf during Operation Desert Storm, receiving a Bronze Star for meritorious service. After six years of military service, he retired as a captain.

His unique experience and visionary leadership is vital to his role in facilitating and leading the companies within the Kahuna Business Group. Frank Lunn has taken on the waves of Hawaii as an amateur surfer – his true passion is challenging others to surf life's waves of change with a Carpe Aqualis! attitude. Lunn is a devoted husband to his wife Lisa and a loving father to their three children Frankie, Matthew and Rachel.

A Special Thank You to St. Jude Children's Research Hospital

"No child should die in the dawn of life."
–**Danny Thomas**, entertainer and founder of St. Jude Children's Research Hospital

What could ever be said or what gift could ever be given to appropriately show your full appreciation for saving the life of your child? To the entire dedicated team of doctors, nurses, technicians, child life, security, scientists, administrators, marketers, photographers, researchers and everyone else associated with this fine institution: *Thank you!*

You saved our son and showed us a face of compassion combined with a purpose for continuing the mission started by Danny Thomas more than forty years ago. With heartfelt gratitude and motivation to see your excellent work continued, we pledge ten percent of all proceeds from *Carpe Aqualis!* and all related Kahuna Empowerment products to be donated to your mission of: *"Finding cures. Saving children."*

Powered by Kahuna Charitable Foundation, a 501(c)(3) not-for-profit corporation

We wish you tremendous continued success and progress!

Sincerely,
Team Kahuna and the family of
Frankie Lunn - Leukemia survivor!

Kahuna Charitable Foundation,
a 501(c)(3) not-for-profit corporation

An Invitation to Share Our Dream

With the publication of our first book, *Stack The Logs!* the entire team at Kahuna got behind the goal to raise $1 million (one day's operating cost for the hospital at the time) for the ongoing work of St. Jude Children's Research Hospital. With progress to that goal and the growth of our business and opportunities, we realized it would only be a beginning.

In 2005, we established the Kahuna Charitable Foundation as a 501(c)(3) not-for-profit corporation with a mission dedicated to adding leverage, value and partnership along with accountability for the fundraising activities of Kahuna Business Group and all subsidiary companies. We are proud to be a corporate partner supporting the mission of St. Jude Children's Research Hospital, and they receive the majority of our support.

Ten percent of all proceeds generated by Kahuna Empowerment, Inc., is joyously donated to St. Jude Children's Research Hospital—Powered by Kahuna Charitable Foundation. This includes all Kahuna Empowerment products and services as well as a growing line of KahunaWear™ with Carpe Aqualis! and Kahuna-branded apparel and merchandise. Please visit the Kahuna General Store at www.KahunaPower.com to see the full product assortment available.

In addition to St. Jude, the Kahuna Charitable Foundation provides us with flexibility to partner with other worthy charitable causes and organizations with other fundraising initiatives. We are very excited for the opportunities to give back and make a difference knowing, "A rising tide lifts all surfboards."

For more information about the work of the Kahuna Charitable Foundation, to make a donation, or to get involved and to share our dream, please visit: www.KahunaCharitable.org or contact me directly at Jamie@KahunaCharitable.org.

Jamie Atchison

– Jamie Atchison,
Executive Director of **Kahuna Charitable Foundation**

St. Jude Children's
Research Hospital
ALSAC • Danny Thomas, Founder
Finding cures. Saving children.

Proud supporter of St. Jude Children's Research Hospital.
10% of all proceeds joyfully donated to St. Jude
through Kahuna Charitable Foundation
- A 501(c)(3) not-for-profit corporation.

Surf -Titude:

"Never turn your back on the waves of change. It is far better to see what is coming so that you can respond or adapt rather than to be blind-sided."

Stay ahead of the waves by signing up for free monthly tips, articles, resources and Surf-Titudes at:

www.KahunaPower.com

Share the Carpe Aqualis!
Seize the Wave Message

Bulk Discounts
Volume discounts are available on orders of ten or more.
Save up to 50% off of the regular retail price.

Custom Publishing
Private label includes a cover with your organization's
name and logo. Information tailored to your needs with
custom audio and training packages highlighting specific
chapters are also available.

Ancillary Products
Workshop outlines, videos, audio, t-shirts and other
products are available for select titles at
www.KahunaPower.com.

Dynamic Speaking
Frank Lunn is available to share his expertise at select
events. See a full list of topics at
www.KahunaPower.com.

Find out more about Kahuna Empowerment, Inc.
products by visiting us online at
www.KahunaPower.com.

Stack The Logs!
Building A Success Framework to Reach Your Dreams

Stack The Logs! is a powerful wake-up call for how to live up to your capabilities and get the most out of life. www.StackTheLogs.com

Written by Frank Lunn, *Stack The Logs!* seamlessly weaves years of priceless knowledge and practical application into an unforgettable story of overcoming hardship to reach success. The five-step S.T.A.C.K. Strategy presents detailed tactics to incrementally overcome procrastination and master the art of tactical goal-setting.

Learn the ten key questions you should be asking yourself to begin each day in a purposeful way. Frank's illuminating words will reveal your great capacity to make a difference in your daily life and in the lives of those around you by giving you the tools and showing you how to use them.

- 320-page **hardcover and softcover**
- **Enhanced e-book** format with live links and resources
- Six power-packed **audio CDs**
- **Companion seventy-five page** *S.T.A.C.K. Plan of Action* – application guide to harness the power of the S.T.A.C.K. Strategy in building a success framework to reach your dreams.

To see the latest package specials visit
www.KahunaPower.com today!

Kahuna Empowerment, Inc. Order Form

Carpe Aqualis! Seize the Wave ___ copies X $14.95 = $_____

Additional Kahuna Empowerment Materials

Carpe Aqualis! Enhanced E-book ___ copies X $29.95 = $_____
Stack The Logs! Hardcover ___ copies X $19.95 = $_____
Stack The Logs! Soft cover ___ copies X $15.95 = $_____
Stack The Logs! Enhanced E-book ___ copies X $29.95 = $_____
Stack The Logs! Audio(6 CDs) ___ copies X $~~69.95~~ 49.95 = $_____
S.T.A.C.K. Plan of Action ___ copies X $29.95 = $_____

Shipping and Handling (see below) $_____
Subtotal $_____
Sales Tax (7.5% – Illinois only) $_____
Total (US Dollars Only) $_____

Shipping and Handling

Total $ Amount	Up to $50	$100-$249	$250-$999	$1000 +
Shipping Cost	$5	$9	$18	$30

Name_____ Email_____

Shipping Address_____ Phone _____

Billing Address_____ Fax_____

City_____ State_____ Zip_____

☐
Please bill my credit card
  Credit Card Number _____ Exp. Date_____
☐ Signature_____
My Check or Money Order for $_____ is enclosed.
  Make checks payable to:

  Kahuna Empowerment, Inc.
  801 W. Chestnut Street, Suite C
  Bloomington, IL 61701

Call your credit card order to: 888-357-8472
or
Order online at www.KahunaPower.com

Fax: 309-829-1680 email: orders@KahunaPower.com

Index